MS-DOS® *6.2*

D0891255

maranGraphics' Development Group

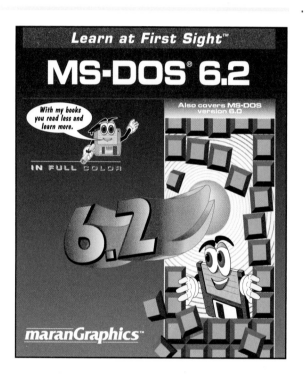

Published in the United States
by Prentice Hall Career & Technology
Englewood Cliffs, New Jersey, 07632

Telephone: 1-800-223-1360
Fax: 1-800-445-6991

Distributed Internationally
by Simon & Schuster

Telephone: 201-767-4990
Fax: 201-767-5625

Distributed in Canada
by Prentice Hall Canada

Telephone: 1-800-567-3800
Fax: 416-299-2529

SINGLE COPY PURCHASES (U.S.)

Telephone: 1-800-947-7700
Fax: 515-284-2607

maranGraphics™ ***Learn at First Sight***™
MS-DOS*® *6.2

Trademark Acknowledgments

Published by Prentice Hall Career & Technology
A Paramount Publishing Company
Englewood Cliffs, New Jersey, 07632

maranGraphics Inc. has attempted to include trademark information for products, services and companies referred to in this guide. Although maranGraphics Inc. has made reasonable efforts in gathering this information, it cannot guarantee its accuracy.

Lotus and 1-2-3 are registered trademarks of Lotus Development Corporation.

Defragmenter, Microsoft Anti-Virus, Microsoft and MS-DOS are registered trademarks of Microsoft Corporation.

The Microsoft Mouse design is a trademark of Microsoft Corporation.

WordPerfect is a registered trademark of WordPerfect Corporation.

Bernoulli is a registered trademark of Iomega Corporation.

©1993
maranGraphics, Inc.

The animated characters are the copyright of maranGraphics, Inc.

Authors:
    Ruth Maran
    Richard Maran

Cover Design and Art Director:
    Jim C. Leung

Illustrator:
    Dave Ross

Screen Production:
    Béla Korcsog

Technical Consultant:
    Eric Feistmantl

Film generated on maranGraphics' Linotronic L-330 imagesetter at 2540 dpi resolution.

Acknowledgments

To Ted Werthman of Prentice Hall Career & Technology for his assistance and creative input.

Special thanks to Alec Saunders and John Hodgins of Microsoft Canada Inc. and Marilyn Meyer for their support and consultation.

To the dedicated staff of maranGraphics, including Mia P. Chao, Saulina DeFrias, Eric Feistmantl, David Hendricks, Béla Korcsog, Jim C. Leung, Judy Maran, Maxine Maran, Robert Maran, Dave Ross and Monica DeVries-Walraven.

Table of Contents

INTRODUCTION

You can describe MS-DOS as your computer's master control program. Like a traffic cop, it keeps everything flowing smoothly.

A collection of programs makes up MS-DOS. They help you:

◆ Manage your files.

◆ Deal with peripheral devices such as your printer.

◆ Control and optimize your computer.

GETTING STARTED	MANAGE DIRECTORIES	MANAGE FILES	MANAGE DISKETTES	MS-DOS SHELL	BACKUP	DATA PROTECTION	DISK MANAGEMENT

INTRODUCTION
START MS-DOS
ENTER A COMMAND
DISPLAY VERSION NUMBER
CLEAR THE SCREEN
CHANGE DATE OR TIME
IMPORTANT KEYS
HELP

What MS-DOS Does

When you first turn on your computer, a small program checks all internal devices, electronic memory and peripherals to ensure they are functioning properly. Once it completes this test, MS-DOS is loaded.

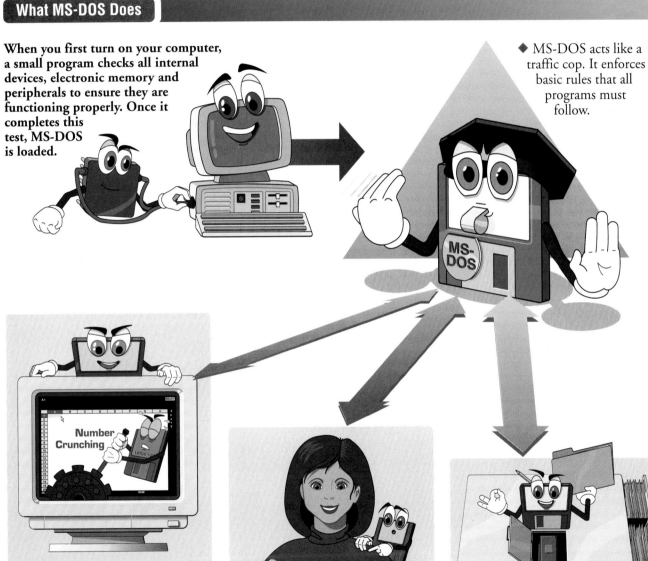

◆ MS-DOS acts like a traffic cop. It enforces basic rules that all programs must follow.

Programs perform tasks such as word processing and spreadsheet analysis. MS-DOS controls how these programs input and output their data.

MS-DOS controls how a program interacts with you.

MS-DOS provides tools to store and organize files and to optimize your computer system.

1 Turn on your computer. It automatically performs a diagnostic check on itself. If the check is OK, the computer beeps once and displays the Command Prompt (C:\>).

◆ Make sure there are no floppy disks in your computer. If there are, the computer will try to start MS-DOS from the floppy drive instead of the hard drive.

INTRODUCTION
START MS-DOS
ENTER A COMMAND
DISPLAY VERSION NUMBER
CLEAR THE SCREEN
CHANGE DATE OR TIME
IMPORTANT KEYS
HELP

The Command Prompt – A text-based way to work with MS-DOS

The command prompt is the most powerful and flexible way of using MS-DOS.

The MS-DOS Shell – A graphic way to work with MS-DOS

The MS-DOS Shell provides an easy, graphic approach to using most MS-DOS commands.

For more information on the MS-DOS Shell, see page 56.

◆ If the MS-DOS Shell is not installed on your computer and you want to use this program, contact your local Microsoft office for ordering information.

5

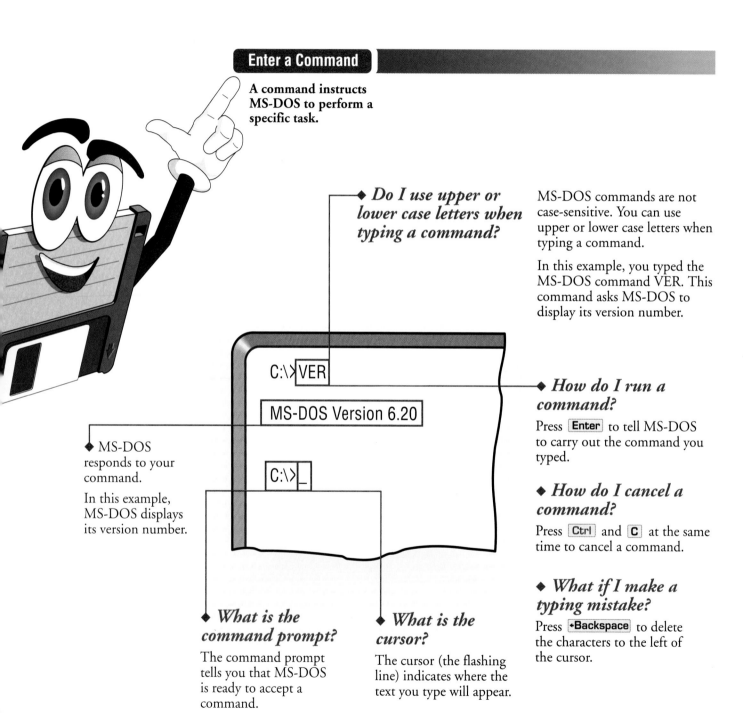

Enter a Command

A command instructs MS-DOS to perform a specific task.

◆ **Do I use upper or lower case letters when typing a command?**

MS-DOS commands are not case-sensitive. You can use upper or lower case letters when typing a command.

In this example, you typed the MS-DOS command VER. This command asks MS-DOS to display its version number.

```
C:\>VER
```

```
MS-DOS Version 6.20
```

```
C:\>_
```

◆ MS-DOS responds to your command.

In this example, MS-DOS displays its version number.

◆ **How do I run a command?**

Press **Enter** to tell MS-DOS to carry out the command you typed.

◆ **How do I cancel a command?**

Press **Ctrl** and **C** at the same time to cancel a command.

◆ **What if I make a typing mistake?**

Press **◆Backspace** to delete the characters to the left of the cursor.

◆ **What is the command prompt?**

The command prompt tells you that MS-DOS is ready to accept a command.

◆ **What is the cursor?**

The cursor (the flashing line) indicates where the text you type will appear.

6

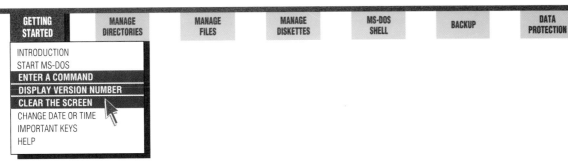

Display the MS-DOS Version Number

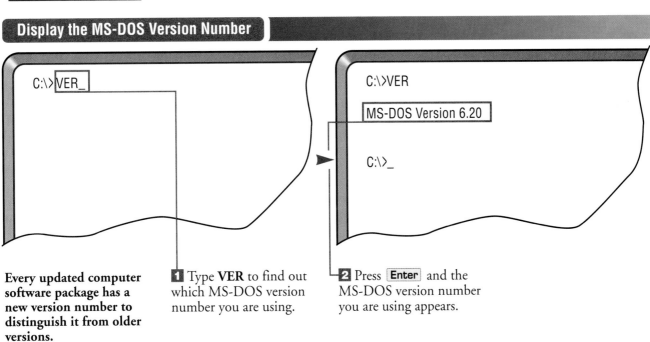

Every updated computer software package has a new version number to distinguish it from older versions.

1 Type **VER** to find out which MS-DOS version number you are using.

2 Press `Enter` and the MS-DOS version number you are using appears.

Clear the Screen

1 Type **CLS** to clear the screen.

2 Press `Enter` and the screen clears.

CHANGE DATE OR TIME

Change the Date

```
C:\>DATE
Current date is Sun 01-24-1993
Enter new date (mm-dd-yy): 02-10-93

C:\>_
```

Check the Date

```
C:\>DATE
Current date is Sun 01-24-1993
Enter new date (mm-dd-yy): 02-10-93

C:\>DATE
Current date is Wed 02-10-1993
Enter new date (mm-dd-yy):

C:\>_
```

1 Type **DATE** and then press **Enter**.

◆ MS-DOS displays what it believes is the current date.

2 If the date is correct, press **Enter**.

3 If the date is incorrect, type the correct date (example: **02-10-93**) and then press **Enter**.

1 Type **DATE** and then press **Enter**.

◆ The new date appears for your verification.

2 Press **Enter** to return to the command prompt.

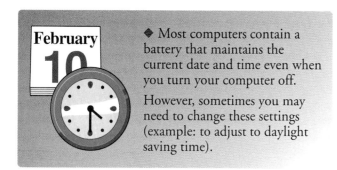

◆ Most computers contain a battery that maintains the current date and time even when you turn your computer off.

However, sometimes you may need to change these settings (example: to adjust to daylight saving time).

Change the Time

```
C:\>TIME
Current time is  4:07:02.52p
Enter new time:  16:30

C:\>_
```

1 Type **TIME** and then press `Enter`.

◆ MS-DOS displays what it believes is the current time.

2 If the time is correct, press `Enter`.

3 If the time is incorrect, type the correct time (example: **16:30**) and then press `Enter`.

*Note: You can type 4:30 p.m. as either **16:30** or **4:30p** (with no spaces between the 0 and p). If you omit the **p**, MS-DOS assumes the time is 4:30 a.m.*

Check the Time

```
C:\>TIME
Current time is  4:07:02.52p
Enter new time:  16:30

C:\>TIME
Current time is  4:30:26.63p
Enter new time:

C:\>_
```

1 Type **TIME** and then press `Enter`.

◆ The new time appears for your verification.

2 Press `Enter` to return to the command prompt.

RESTART MS-DOS

You may need to restart your computer if it is not responding properly or if the keyboard locks.

METHOD 1

◆ **This method is called a "warm boot."** Hold down `Ctrl` and `Alt` while you press `Delete`.

◆ The screen clears and MS-DOS reloads into the computer.

METHOD 2

◆ **Use this method only if Method 1 does not work**. Press the **Reset** button located on the front of your computer, or turn the computer off, wait three seconds and then turn it on.

IMPORTANT KEYS

The computer remembers the last MS-DOS command you typed. You can recall or modify the command using the F1, F2 or F3 function keys.

◆ F1 KEY

Press the `F1` key to display the last command you typed, one character at a time.

◆ F2 KEY

Press the `F2` key to display the last command you typed, up to a specified character. For example, if the last command you typed was ABCDEFGH and you press `F2` and then `E`, the screen will display ABCD.

◆ F3 KEY

Press the `F3` key to display the last command you typed.

◆ ESCAPE KEY

Press the `Esc` key to cancel a line of text you typed.

◆ CAPITALS LOCK

Press the `Caps Lock` key to switch the keys between upper (ABCD) and lower case (abcd) letters.

◆ SHIFT KEY

If you press the `Shift` key in combination with another key, you can change the case of a letter (example: **a** to **A**) or type a special character (example: **$**).

◆ ALTERNATE KEY

The `Alt` key works in combination with other keys to select MS-DOS Shell commands.

◆ SPACEBAR

Press the **Spacebar** to insert a blank space.

◆ BACKSPACE KEY

Press the ⬅Backspace key to erase the character to the left of the cursor.

◆ STATUS INDICATORS

These lights are "lit" when special keyboard switches are turned on. For example, when you press the Num Lock key, the **Num Lock** light comes on.

◆ NUMERIC LOCK

Press the Num Lock key to switch the keys in the numeric keypad between cursor movement and number keys.

◆ ENTER KEY

Press the Enter key to tell MS-DOS to carry out the command you typed.

◆ CONTROL KEY

The Ctrl key works in combination with other keys. For example, to cancel a command, press the Ctrl and C keys at the same time.

◆ NUMERIC KEYPAD/ARROW KEYS

When the **Num Lock** light is on, you can use the numbers 0 through 9 and the decimal point to quickly enter numbers.

When the **Num Lock** light is off, you can use the arrow keys to move the cursor.

HELP

MS-DOS Help provides a complete glossary of MS-DOS commands. If you cannot remember how to perform a task, look up the command for an explanation.

General Help

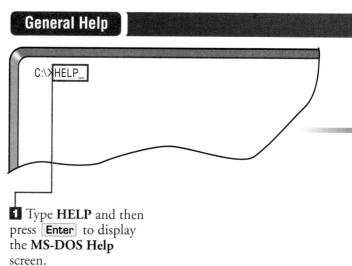

C:\>HELP_

1 Type **HELP** and then press **Enter** to display the **MS-DOS Help** screen.

Specific Help

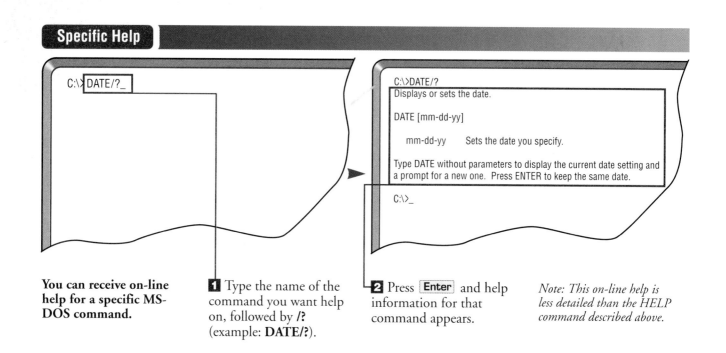

C:\>DATE/?_

C:\>DATE/?
Displays or sets the date.

DATE [mm-dd-yy]

   mm-dd-yy   Sets the date you specify.

Type DATE without parameters to display the current date setting and a prompt for a new one. Press ENTER to keep the same date.

C:\>_

You can receive on-line help for a specific MS-DOS command.

1 Type the name of the command you want help on, followed by **/?** (example: **DATE/?**).

2 Press **Enter** and help information for that command appears.

Note: This on-line help is less detailed than the HELP command described above.

2 Use the ↓, ↑ and **Tab** keys to position the cursor on the command you want help on (example: **Cd**).

Note: The cursor is the flashing line (_).

3 Press **Enter** and help information for that command appears.

4 To exit MS-DOS Help and return to the command prompt, press **Alt**, **F**, **X**.

▼ **Notes** displays additional information on the command.

▼ **Examples** displays ways to use the command.

To display either screen, press **Tab** until the cursor is on the heading and then press **Enter**.

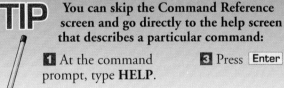

TIP You can skip the Command Reference screen and go directly to the help screen that describes a particular command:

1 At the command prompt, type **HELP**.

2 Press the **Spacebar** and then type the command name (example: **Cd**).

3 Press **Enter**.

13

INTRODUCTION
TO DRIVES

What are Drives?

◆ Your computer stores your programs and data in devices called "drives." A drive is similar to a filing cabinet because it stores information in an organized way.

◆ Most computers have one hard drive and one or two floppy drives. The hard drive is usually called drive C. The floppy drives are called drives A and B.

Hard drive (C:)

◆ A hard drive stores your programs and data. Most computers have at least one hard drive. This drive is called drive **C**.

Note: Some computers may have additional drives, depending on their setup.

Floppy drives (A: and B:)

◆ Floppy drives store your programs and data on removable media called diskettes (or floppy disks). Diskettes operate slower and store less data than hard drives.

If a computer has only one floppy drive, it is called drive **A**.

If a computer has two floppy drives, the second drive is called drive **B**.

TIP DRIVE NAME

C: ─◆ A drive name consists of two parts: the letter and a colon (:). The colon represents the word "drive." For example, typing **C:** refers to the **C drive**.

What is the Current Drive?

`C:\>_`

◆ MS-DOS displays the current drive on the computer screen. In this example, the current drive is **C:**.

When entering a command, type the drive name (example: **C:**). This tells MS-DOS which drive you want to work with. If you leave out the drive name, MS-DOS assumes you want the command to work with the current drive.

To simplify the typing of MS-DOS commands:

Make sure the current drive is:

C:	**A:**	**B:**
When you want a command to work with the **C drive**.	When you want a command to work with the **A drive**.	When you want a command to work with the **B drive**.

Change Drives

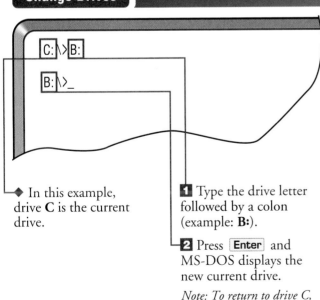

`C:\>B:`

`B:\>_`

◆ In this example, drive **C** is the current drive.

1 Type the drive letter followed by a colon (example: **B:**).

2 Press **Enter** and MS-DOS displays the new current drive.

*Note: To return to drive C, type **C:** and then press **Enter**.*

Before changing to a floppy drive, make sure you insert a diskette into the drive.

Note: For more information on floppy drives and diskettes, refer to page 50.

INTRODUCTION TO DIRECTORIES

Directories are similar to the drawers and folders in a filing cabinet. They help you organize the programs and data stored on your computer.

◆ **Floppy drives (A: and B:)**
◆ **Hard drive (C:)**

◆ **Root directory**

The main directory is called the root directory. All other directories are located below this directory.

◆ **Directories**

Each directory usually contains related information. For example, you can create a **DATA** directory to hold all your data files.

◆ **Subdirectories**

Each drawer can contain folders called subdirectories. A subdirectory can store files or other subdirectories.

◆ **Files**

A file is a document stored in a directory. A unique name identifies each file.

INTRODUCTION TO DRIVES
INTRODUCTION TO DIRECTORIES
MAKE A DIRECTORY
CHANGE DIRECTORIES
DISPLAY DIRECTORY TREE
REMOVE A DIRECTORY

What is a Path?

If you require a certain file, you must tell MS-DOS exactly how to find it. A "path" is the direction you tell MS-DOS to follow to locate that file.

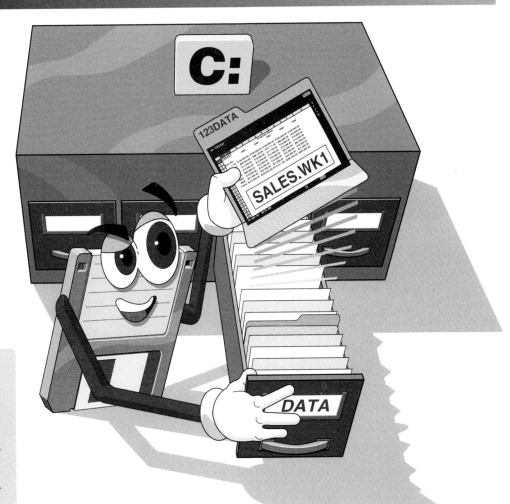

For example, to find the SALES.WK1 file, you must:

Go to *the drawer labeled* **DATA**

Go to *the folder labeled* **123DATA**

Go to *the file labeled* **SALES.WK1**

Go to equals \

To instruct MS-DOS to retrieve the same file stored on your hard drive, replace the words Go to with \.

To retrieve this file, you must type:

\DATA\123DATA\SALES.WK1

17

MAKE A DIRECTORY

Make a Directory

The Make Directory command (typed as MD) lets you create a new directory.

Directories help you organize the programs and data stored on your hard and floppy drives.

The Make Directory command is:

MD **DRIVE** **PATH** **DIRECTORY NAME**

MD	Stands for Make Directory.
DRIVE	Tells MS-DOS the drive where you want to create the new directory.
PATH	Tells MS-DOS the path to the new directory.
DIRECTORY NAME	Tells MS-DOS the name of the new directory.

```
C:\>MD \DATA

C:\>_
```

Make the DATA directory

1 Type **MD** (for Make Directory) and then press the **Spacebar**.

2 Type the name of the new directory (example: **\DATA**).

3 Press **Enter** and the command prompt **C:\>** appears, indicating that MS-DOS created the directory.

TIP ◆ If you omit the drive and path, directories are created in the current drive and within the current directory.

In this example, the DATA directory is created one level below the root directory. You can use this directory to separate your data files from your program files. This makes it more efficient when working with a lot of information.

| GETTING STARTED | MANAGE DIRECTORIES | MANAGE FILES | MANAGE DISKETTES | MS-DOS SHELL | BACKUP | DATA PROTECTION | DISK MANAGEMENT |

INTRODUCTION TO DRIVES
INTRODUCTION TO DIRECTORIES
MAKE A DIRECTORY
CHANGE DIRECTORIES
DISPLAY DIRECTORY TREE
REMOVE A DIRECTORY

```
C:\> MD \DATA\123DATA
C:\>_
```

```
C:\> MD \DATA\WPDATA
C:\>_
```

Make the 123DATA directory

1 Type **MD** (for **M**ake **D**irectory) and then press the **Spacebar**.

2 Type the path to the directory you want to create, followed by the name of the new directory (example: **\DATA\123DATA**).

3 Press **Enter** and the command prompt **C:\>** appears, indicating that MS-DOS created the directory.

Make the WPDATA directory

1 Type **MD** (for **M**ake **D**irectory) and then press the **Spacebar**.

2 Type the path to the directory you want to create, followed by the name of the new directory (example: **\DATA\WPDATA**).

3 Press **Enter** and the command prompt **C:\>** appears, indicating that MS-DOS created the directory.

In this example, the 123DATA directory is created one level below the DATA directory. You can store all your spreadsheet files in this directory.

In this example, the WPDATA directory is created one level below the DATA directory. You can store all your word processing files in this directory.

CHANGE DIRECTORIES

The Change Directory command (typed as CD) allows you to navigate through your directory structure.

The Change Directory command is:

`CD` `PATH`

CD	Stands for Change Directory.
PATH	Tells MS-DOS the path to the directory you want to change to.

Change the Current Directory

In this example, the current directory is changed from the root directory to the 123DATA directory.

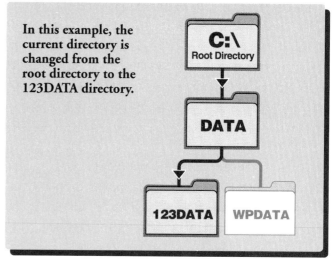

Move Up One Directory Level (Shortcut)

In this example, the current directory is changed from the 123DATA directory to the DATA directory.

This is a fast method of moving up the directory structure one level at a time.

1 Type **CD..** and then press `Enter`.

◆ The command prompt appears displaying the new current directory.

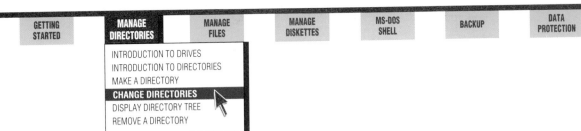

GETTING STARTED | MANAGE DIRECTORIES | MANAGE FILES | MANAGE DISKETTES | MS-DOS SHELL | BACKUP | DATA PROTECTION | DISK MANAGEMENT

INTRODUCTION TO DRIVES
INTRODUCTION TO DIRECTORIES
MAKE A DIRECTORY
CHANGE DIRECTORIES
DISPLAY DIRECTORY TREE
REMOVE A DIRECTORY

```
C:\>CD \DATA\123DATA

C:\DATA\123DATA>_
```

1 Type **CD** (for **C**hange **D**irectory) and then press the **Spacebar**.

2 Type the path to the directory you want to change to (example: **\DATA\123DATA**).

3 Press **Enter** and the command prompt appears displaying the new current directory.

Move Down One Directory Level (Shortcut)

In this example, the current directory is changed from the DATA directory to the WPDATA directory.

This is a fast method of moving down the directory structure one level at a time.

```
C:\DATA>CD WPDATA

C:\DATA\WPDATA>_
```

1 Type **CD** (for **C**hange **D**irectory) and then press the **Spacebar**.

2 Type the name of the directory you want to change to (example: **WPDATA**).

3 Press **Enter** and the command prompt appears displaying the new current directory.

*Note: To change from any directory to the root directory, type **CD** and then press* **Enter**.

DISPLAY DIRECTORY TREE

The Tree command visually displays the structure of a directory's contents. This command is extremely helpful if you cannot remember how your directories are organized.

The Tree command is:

TREE `DRIVE` `PATH` `/F`

DRIVE	Tells MS-DOS the drive that contains the directory structure you want to display.
PATH	Tells MS-DOS where to start displaying the directory structure.
/F	Tells MS-DOS to list all files in the displayed directories.

Note: If you omit the drive and path, MS-DOS displays a directory structure of the current drive, starting from the current directory.

Display Only Directories

In this example, all directories starting from the root directory (C:\) are displayed.

PRINT A DIRECTORY STRUCTURE

◆ Type **>PRN** after the **TREE** command to direct the output to your printer instead of the screen.

For example, to print the directory structure of the DOS directory, including all files, type:

TREE \DOS/F>PRN

Note: Refer to your printer manual to determine if your printer supports the extended character set. If it does not, type /A after the Tree command (example: TREE \DOS/F/A>PRN). This adds vertical bars, hyphens, etc. to help your printer draw the directory structure.

Display Files and Directories

In this example, all subdirectories and files starting from the DOS directory are displayed.

INTRODUCTION TO DRIVES
INTRODUCTION TO DIRECTORIES
MAKE A DIRECTORY
CHANGE DIRECTORIES
DISPLAY DIRECTORY TREE
REMOVE A DIRECTORY

1 Type **TREE** and then press the **Spacebar**.

2 Type the path to the directory where you want to start displaying the directory structure (example: \).

Note: The \ symbol represents the root directory of the drive.

3 Press **Enter** and the directory structure appears. MS-DOS displays all subdirectories starting from the directory you specified.

1 Type **TREE** and then press the **Spacebar**.

2 Type the path to the directory where you want to start displaying the directory structure (example: **\DOS**).

3 Type **/F** (for **F**iles) to show the names of the files in each directory.

4 If you expect the screen display to fill more than one screen, hold down **Shift** and press **** to add ¦ to the command. Then type **MORE**.

*Note: **MORE** stops the display each time the information fills up the screen.*

5 Press **Enter** and the directory structure appears. MS-DOS displays all subdirectories and files starting from the directory you specified.

Note: In this example, the DOS directory contains no subdirectories.

6 If the screen display exceeds one screen, press **Enter** to display the next screen. Continue pressing **Enter** until you have viewed all the files.

23

REMOVE A DIRECTORY

Remove a Directory

The Remove Directory command (typed as RD) allows you to remove empty directories from your drive.

The Remove Directory command is:

RD	DRIVE	PATH

RD	Stands for Remove Directory.
DRIVE	Tells MS-DOS the drive that contains the directory you want to remove.
PATH	Tells MS-DOS the path to the directory you want to remove.

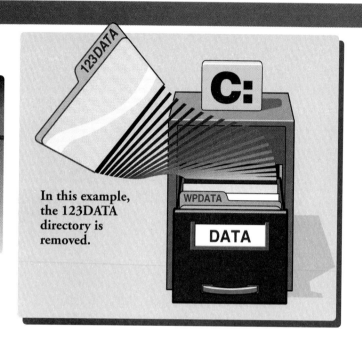

In this example, the 123DATA directory is removed.

TIP

◆ If you omit the drive, MS-DOS assumes the current drive contains the directory you want to remove.

C:\>RD \DATA\123DATA_

C:\>RD \DATA\123DATA

C:\>_

1 Type **RD** (for **R**emove **D**irectory) and then press the **Spacebar**.

2 Type the path to the directory you want to remove (example: **\DATA\123DATA**).

3 Press **Enter** and the command prompt **C:\>** appears, indicating that MS-DOS removed the directory.

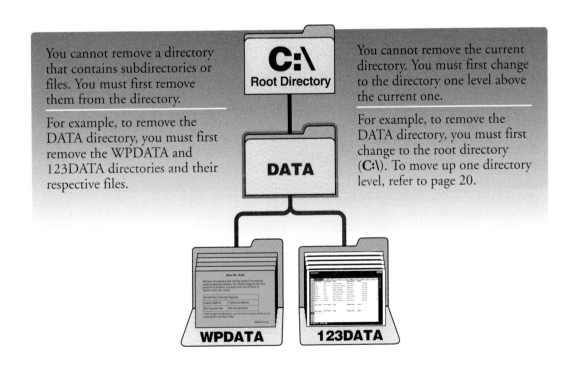

You cannot remove a directory that contains subdirectories or files. You must first remove them from the directory.

For example, to remove the DATA directory, you must first remove the WPDATA and 123DATA directories and their respective files.

You cannot remove the current directory. You must first change to the directory one level above the current one.

For example, to remove the DATA directory, you must first change to the root directory (**C:**). To move up one directory level, refer to page 20.

C:
Root Directory

DATA

WPDATA   **123DATA**

INTRODUCTION TO FILES

What is a File?

A file is a named collection of information stored on a disk.

PROGRAM FILES

Program files enable you to write letters, analyze numbers, sort data, draw pictures and even play games.

DATA FILES

Data files are documents you create using program files.

File Location

If you require a certain file, you must tell MS-DOS exactly how to find it. A "path" is the direction you tell MS-DOS to follow to locate that file.

IN EVERYDAY LANGUAGE...

To find the **PROJECT3.WK1** file, you must:

Go to the drawer labeled **DATA**, then

Go to the folder labeled **123DATA**, then

Go to the file labeled **PROJECT3.WK1**

Go to equals ****

IN COMPUTER LANGUAGE...

To retrieve the **PROJECT3.WK1** file, you must type:

\DATA\123DATA\PROJECT3.WK1

INTRODUCTION TO FILES
INTRODUCTION TO WILDCARDS
DIRECTORY CONTENTS
SORT FILES
SEARCH FOR FILES

COPY FILES
MOVE FILES
RENAME FILES
DELETE FILES

File Names

A file name consists of two parts: the name and the extension. You must separate these parts with a period.

PROJECT3 . WK1

◆ Period
A period must separate the name and the extension.

◆ Name
The name describes the contents of a file. It can have up to 8 characters.

◆ Extension
The extension describes the type of information a file contains. It can have up to 3 characters.

FILE NAME RULES

The following characters are allowed:

◆ The letters A to Z, upper or lower case

◆ The numbers 0 through 9

◆ The symbols _ ^ $ ~ ! # % & - { } @ ' ( )

◆ The file name cannot contain a period, blank space or comma

◆ Each file in a directory must have a unique name.

INVALID FILE NAMES

MY WORK.TXT — A file name cannot contain any spaces.

LETTERTOROB.LET — A file name cannot contain more than eight characters before the period.

MEMO\WED.DOC — A file name cannot contain the \ character.

COMMON EXTENSIONS

Program and data files normally have unique extensions to distinguish their files from others.

Word Processing Files
.TXT
.LET
.DOC

Spreadsheet Files
.WK3
.WK1
.XLS

Program Files
.BAT
.COM
.EXE

INTRODUCTION TO WILDCARDS

What are Wildcards?

You can use wildcards with certain commands to enable you to work with several files at the same time.

There are two wildcards: the asterisk (*) and the question mark (?).

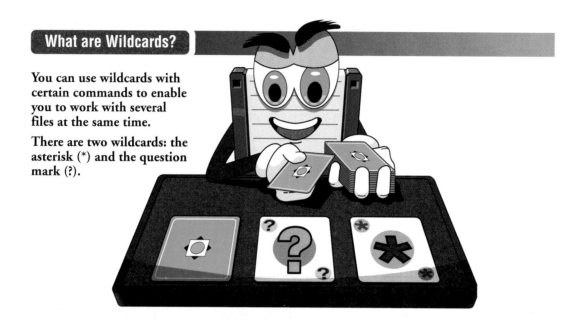

Using the * Wildcard

The asterisk (*) represents one or more characters in a file name.

MEMO.* includes all files named MEMO, with any extension

*.LET includes all files with the LET extension

A*.* includes all files starting with the letter A, with any extension

. includes all files

| GETTING STARTED | MANAGE DIRECTORIES | MANAGE FILES | MANAGE DISKETTES | MS-DOS SHELL | BACKUP | DATA PROTECTION | DISK MANAGEMENT |

INTRODUCTION TO FILES
INTRODUCTION TO WILDCARDS
DIRECTORY CONTENTS
SORT FILES
SEARCH FOR FILES

COPY FILES
MOVE FILES
RENAME FILES
DELETE FILES

Using the ? Wildcard

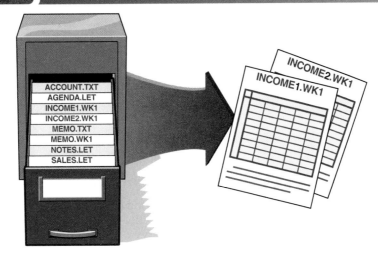

The question mark (?) represents a single character in a file name.

ACCOUNT.TXT
AGENDA.LET
INCOME1.WK1
INCOME2.WK1
MEMO.TXT
MEMO.WK1
NOTES.LET
SALES.LET

INCOME2.WK1
INCOME1.WK1

INCOME?.WK1 includes all files starting with INCOME, followed by any character and then .WK1

CREATING PRACTICE FILES

Normally, you create files using application software such as word processors or spreadsheets. You should only use this method to create practice files.

C:
Root Directory

DATA

123DATA   WPDATA

```
C:\>CD \DATA\123DATA

C:\DATA\123DATA>COPY CON INCOME1Q.WK1
ABCDE^Z
        1 file(s) copied

C:\DATA\123DATA>_
```

1 Change to the directory where you want the file to reside (example: type **CD** (for Change **D**irectory) and then press the **Spacebar**. Type **\DATA\123DATA** and then press **Enter**).

2 Type **COPY** and then press the **Spacebar**. Type **CON** and then press the **Spacebar**.

3 Type the name of the file you want to create (example: **INCOME1Q.WK1**) and then press **Enter**.

4 Type any character(s) (example: **ABCDE**). Each character you type represents one byte.

5 Press **F6**. The characters **^Z** appear.

6 Press **Enter** to create the file.

DIRECTORY CONTENTS

The Directory command (typed as DIR) lists all the subdirectories and files within a directory. It also displays the size of the files and the date and time they were last modified.

Use this command if you cannot remember the contents of a particular directory.

The Directory command is:

DIR	DRIVE	PATH

DIR Stands for DIRectory.

DRIVE Tells MS-DOS the drive containing the directory whose contents you want to display.

PATH Tells MS-DOS the path to the directory whose contents you want to display.

Note: If you omit the drive and path, MS-DOS displays the subdirectories and files of the current drive and directory.

TO DISPLAY ONLY DIRECTORIES

Type **/AD** after the **DIR** command.

For example, to display only the directories in the DOS directory, type: **DIR \DOS /AD**

TO DISPLAY ONLY FILES

Type **/A-D** after the **DIR** command.

For example, to display only the files in the DOS directory, type: **DIR \DOS /A-D**

TO PRINT THE CONTENTS OF A DIRECTORY

Type **>PRN** after the **DIR** command.

For example, to print the contents of the DOS directory, type: **DIR \DOS >PRN**

C:\> DIR \DATA\123DATA_

1 Type **DIR** (for **DIR**ectory) and then press the **Spacebar**.

2 Type the path to the directory whose contents you want to display (example: **\DATA\123DATA**).

3 Press **Enter** and the contents of the directory appear.

C:
Root Directory

DATA

123DATA

In this example, the contents of the 123DATA directory are displayed.

INTRODUCTION TO FILES
INTRODUCTION TO WILDCARDS
DIRECTORY CONTENTS
SORT FILES
SEARCH FOR FILES

COPY FILES
MOVE FILES
RENAME FILES
DELETE FILES

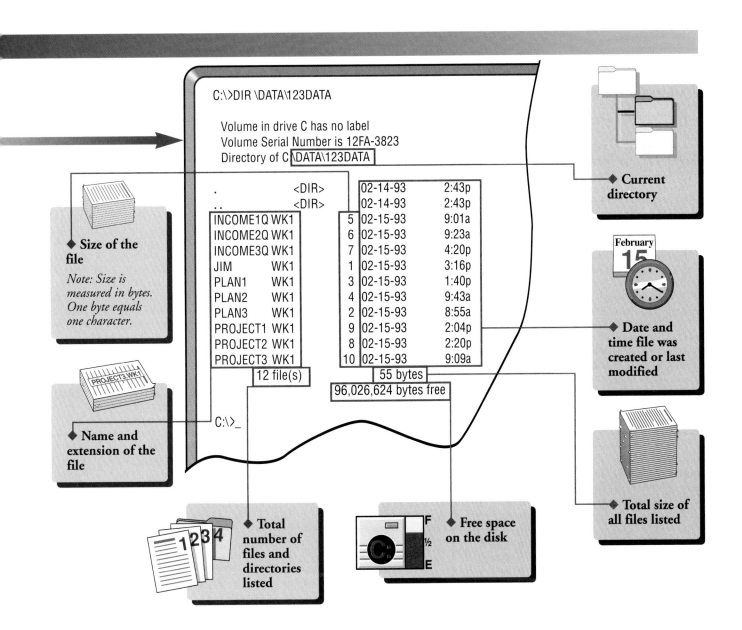

C:\>DIR \DATA\123DATA

Volume in drive C has no label
Volume Serial Number is 12FA-3823
Directory of C:\DATA\123DATA

.	<DIR>		02-14-93	2:43p
..	<DIR>		02-14-93	2:43p
INCOME1Q WK1		5	02-15-93	9:01a
INCOME2Q WK1		6	02-15-93	9:23a
INCOME3Q WK1		7	02-15-93	4:20p
JIM WK1		1	02-15-93	3:16p
PLAN1 WK1		3	02-15-93	1:40p
PLAN2 WK1		4	02-15-93	9:43a
PLAN3 WK1		2	02-15-93	8:55a
PROJECT1 WK1		9	02-15-93	2:04p
PROJECT2 WK1		8	02-15-93	2:20p
PROJECT3 WK1		10	02-15-93	9:09a
	12 file(s)	55 bytes		
	96,026,624 bytes free			

C:\>_

◆ **Current directory**

◆ **Size of the file**

Note: Size is measured in bytes. One byte equals one character.

◆ **Name and extension of the file**

◆ **Date and time file was created or last modified**

◆ **Total size of all files listed**

◆ **Total number of files and directories listed**

◆ **Free space on the disk**

DIRECTORY CONTENTS

If you cannot view the entire contents of a directory on one screen, MS-DOS offers two options.

WIDE DISPLAY

Displays the contents of a directory in a wide format, excluding the file size and creation date and time.

PAUSE DISPLAY

Displays the contents of a directory one screen at a time.

◆ Files not displayed on the screen.

Wide Display

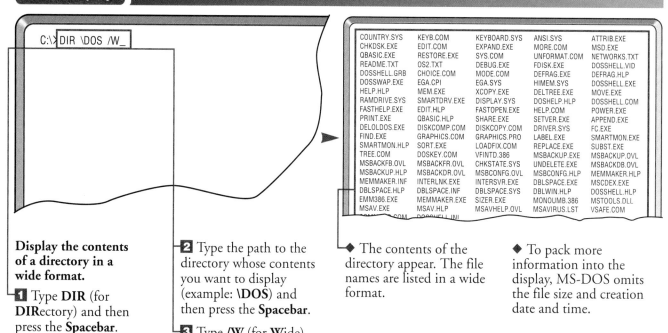

C:\>DIR \DOS /W_

COUNTRY.SYS	KEYB.COM	KEYBOARD.SYS	ANSI.SYS	ATTRIB.EXE
CHKDSK.EXE	EDIT.COM	EXPAND.EXE	MORE.COM	MSD.EXE
QBASIC.EXE	RESTORE.EXE	SYS.COM	UNFORMAT.COM	NETWORKS.TXT
README.TXT	OS2.TXT	DEBUG.EXE	FDISK.EXE	DOSSHELL.VID
DOSSHELL.GRB	CHOICE.COM	MODE.COM	DEFRAG.EXE	DEFRAG.HLP
DOSSWAP.EXE	EGA.CPI	EGA.SYS	HIMEM.SYS	DOSSHELL.EXE
HELP.HLP	MEM.EXE	XCOPY.EXE	DELTREE.EXE	MOVE.EXE
RAMDRIVE.SYS	SMARTDRV.EXE	DISPLAY.SYS	DOSHELP.HLP	DOSSHELL.COM
FASTHELP.EXE	EDIT.HLP	FASTOPEN.EXE	HELP.COM	POWER.EXE
PRINT.EXE	QBASIC.HLP	SHARE.EXE	SETVER.EXE	APPEND.EXE
DELOLDOS.EXE	DISKCOMP.COM	DISKCOPY.COM	DRIVER.SYS	FC.EXE
FIND.EXE	GRAPHICS.COM	GRAPHICS.PRO	LABEL.EXE	SMARTMON.EXE
SMARTMON.HLP	SORT.EXE	LOADFIX.COM	REPLACE.EXE	SUBST.EXE
TREE.COM	DOSKEY.COM	VFINTD.386	MSBACKUP.EXE	MSBACKUP.OVL
MSBACKFB.OVL	MSBACKFR.OVL	CHKSTATE.SYS	UNDELETE.EXE	MSBACKDB.OVL
MSBACKUP.HLP	MSBACKDR.OVL	MSBCONFG.OVL	MSBCONFG.HLP	MEMMAKER.HLP
MEMMAKER.INF	INTERLNK.EXE	INTERSVR.EXE	DBLSPACE.EXE	MSCDEX.EXE
DBLSPACE.HLP	DBLSPACE.INF	DBLSPACE.SYS	DBLWIN.HLP	DOSSHELL.HLP
EMM386.EXE	MEMMAKER.EXE	SIZER.EXE	MONOUMB.386	MSTOOLS.DLL
MSAV.EXE	MSAV.HLP	MSAVHELP.OVL	MSAVIRUS.LST	VSAFE.COM

Display the contents of a directory in a wide format.

1 Type **DIR** (for **DIR**ectory) and then press the **Spacebar**.

2 Type the path to the directory whose contents you want to display (example: **\DOS**) and then press the **Spacebar**.

3 Type **/W** (for **W**ide) and then press `Enter`.

◆ The contents of the directory appear. The file names are listed in a wide format.

◆ To pack more information into the display, MS-DOS omits the file size and creation date and time.

GETTING STARTED | MANAGE DIRECTORIES | MANAGE FILES | MANAGE DISKETTES | MS-DOS SHELL | BACKUP | DATA PROTECTION | DISK MANAGEMENT

INTRODUCTION TO FILES
INTRODUCTION TO WILDCARDS
DIRECTORY CONTENTS
SORT FILES
SEARCH FOR FILES

COPY FILES
MOVE FILES
RENAME FILES
DELETE FILES

Pause Display

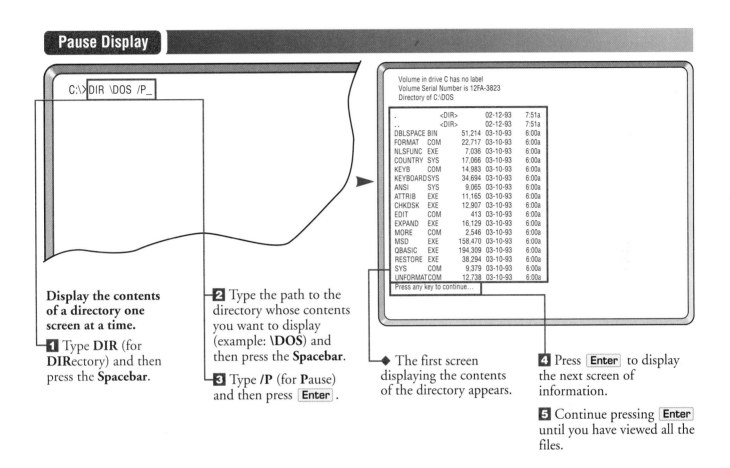

Display the contents of a directory one screen at a time.

1 Type **DIR** (for **DIR**ectory) and then press the **Spacebar**.

2 Type the path to the directory whose contents you want to display (example: **\DOS**) and then press the **Spacebar**.

3 Type **/P** (for **P**ause) and then press Enter.

◆ The first screen displaying the contents of the directory appears.

4 Press Enter to display the next screen of information.

5 Continue pressing Enter until you have viewed all the files.

You can combine the Wide and Pause display options.

◆ Type **/W /P** after the **DIR** command.

For example, to display the contents of the **DOS** directory using both the **Wide** and **Pause** display options, type:
DIR \DOS /W /P

DIRECTORY CONTENTS

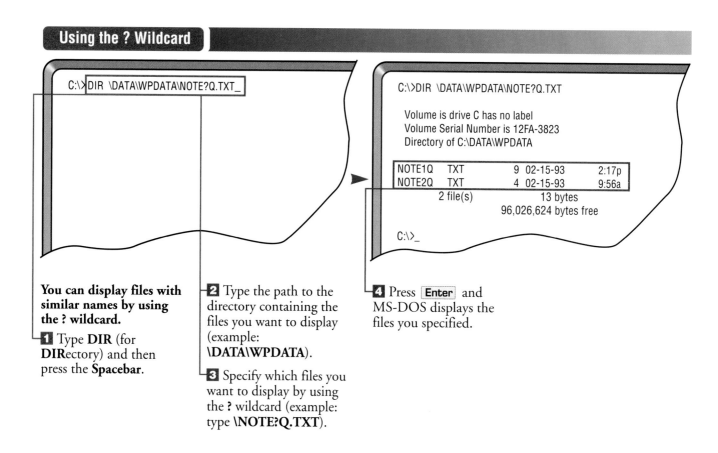

```
C:\>DIR \DATA\WPDATA\NOTE?Q.TXT_
```

```
C:\>DIR \DATA\WPDATA\NOTE?Q.TXT

Volume is drive C has no label
Volume Serial Number is 12FA-3823
Directory of C:\DATA\WPDATA

NOTE1Q    TXT        9  02-15-93      2:17p
NOTE2Q    TXT        4  02-15-93      9:56a
        2 file(s)            13 bytes
                  96,026,624 bytes free

C:\>_
```

You can display files with similar names by using the ? wildcard.

1 Type **DIR** (for **DIR**ectory) and then press the **Spacebar**.

2 Type the path to the directory containing the files you want to display (example: **\DATA\WPDATA**).

3 Specify which files you want to display by using the **?** wildcard (example: type **\NOTE?Q.TXT**).

4 Press **Enter** and MS-DOS displays the files you specified.

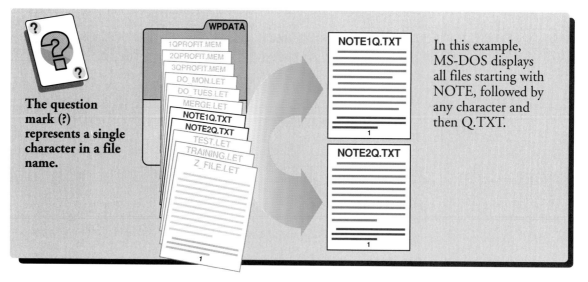

The question mark (?) represents a single character in a file name.

In this example, MS-DOS displays all files starting with NOTE, followed by any character and then Q.TXT.

| GETTING STARTED | MANAGE DIRECTORIES | MANAGE FILES | MANAGE DISKETTES | MS-DOS SHELL | BACKUP | DATA PROTECTION | DISK MANAGEMENT |

INTRODUCTION TO FILES
INTRODUCTION TO WILDCARDS
DIRECTORY CONTENTS
SORT FILES
SEARCH FOR FILES

COPY FILES
MOVE FILES
RENAME FILES
DELETE FILES

Using the * Wildcard

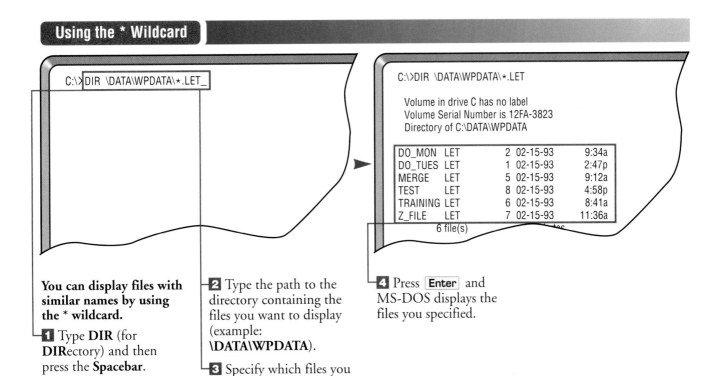

C:\>DIR \DATA\WPDATA*.LET_

C:\>DIR \DATA\WPDATA*.LET

Volume in drive C has no label
Volume Serial Number is 12FA-3823
Directory of C:\DATA\WPDATA

DO_MON	LET	2	02-15-93	9:34a
DO_TUES	LET	1	02-15-93	2:47p
MERGE	LET	5	02-15-93	9:12a
TEST	LET	8	02-15-93	4:58p
TRAINING	LET	6	02-15-93	8:41a
Z_FILE	LET	7	02-15-93	11:36a

6 file(s)

You can display files with similar names by using the * wildcard.

1 Type **DIR** (for **DIR**ectory) and then press the **Spacebar**.

2 Type the path to the directory containing the files you want to display (example: **\DATA\WPDATA**).

3 Specify which files you want to display by using the * wildcard (example: type ***.LET**).

4 Press **Enter** and MS-DOS displays the files you specified.

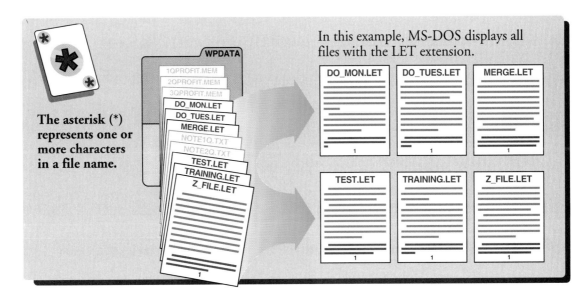

The asterisk (*) represents one or more characters in a file name.

WPDATA

1QPROFIT.MEM
2QPROFIT.MEM
3QPROFIT.MEM
DO_MON.LET
DO_TUES.LET
MERGE.LET
NOTE1Q.TXT
NOTE2Q.TXT
TEST.LET
TRAINING.LET
Z_FILE.LET

In this example, MS-DOS displays all files with the LET extension.

| DO_MON.LET | DO_TUES.LET | MERGE.LET |
| TEST.LET | TRAINING.LET | Z_FILE.LET |

SORT FILES

Sort Files by Extension (A to Z)

`C:\> DIR \DATA\WPDATA /OE_`

1 Type **DIR** (for **DIR**ectory) and then press the **Spacebar**.

2 Type the path to the directory containing the files you want to sort (example: **\DATA\WPDATA**) and then press the **Spacebar**.

3 Type **/OE** (for **O**rder by **E**xtension).

Note: To sort your files by extension (Z to A), type /O-E

```
C:\>DIR \DATA\WPDATA /OE

  Volume in drive C has no label
  Volume Serial Number is 12FA-3823
  Directory of C:\DATA\WPDATA

  .            <DIR>        02-14-93    2:43p
  ..           <DIR>        02-14-93    2:43p
  DO_MON   LET      2       02-15-93    9:34a
  DO_TUES  LET      1       02-15-93    2:47p
  MERGE    LET      5       02-15-93    9:12a
  TEST     LET      8       02-15-93    4:58p
  TRAINING LET      6       02-15-93    8:41a
  Z_FILE   LET      7       02-15-93   11:36a
  1QPROFIT MEM     10       02-15-93    1:59p
  2QPROFIT MEM     11       02-15-93    9:03a
  3QPROFIT MEM      3       02-15-93    3:22p
  NOTE1Q   TXT      9       02-15-93    2:17p
  NOTE2Q   TXT      4       02-15-93    9:56a
       13 file(s)          66 bytes
                 96,026,624 bytes free
```

4 Press **Enter** to display the files sorted by extension.

Sort Files by Name (A to Z)

`C:\> DIR \DATA\WPDATA /ON_`

1 Type **DIR** (for **DIR**ectory) and then press the **Spacebar**.

2 Type the path to the directory containing the files you want to sort (example: **\DATA\WPDATA**) and then press the **Spacebar**.

3 Type **/ON** (for **O**rder by **N**ame).

Note: To sort your files by name (Z to A), type /O-N

```
C:\>DIR \DATA\WPDATA /ON

  Volume in drive C has no label
  Volume Serial Number is 12FA-3823
  Directory of C:\DATA\WPDATA

  .            <DIR>        02-14-93    2:43p
  ..           <DIR>        02-14-93    2:43p
  1QPROFIT MEM     10       02-15-93    1:59p
  2QPROFIT MEM     11       02-15-93    9:03a
  3QPROFIT MEM      3       02-15-93    3:22p
  DO_MON   LET      2       02-15-93    9:34a
  DO_TUES  LET      1       02-15-93    2:47p
  MERGE    LET      5       02-15-93    9:12a
  NOTE1Q   TXT      9       02-15-93    2:17p
  NOTE2Q   TXT      4       02-15-93    9:56a
  TEST     LET      8       02-15-93    4:58p
  TRAINING LET      6       02-15-93    8:41a
  Z_FILE   LET      7       02-15-93   11:36a
       13 file(s)          66 bytes
                 96,026,624 bytes free
```

4 Press **Enter** to display the files sorted by name.

INTRODUCTION TO FILES
INTRODUCTION TO WILDCARDS
DIRECTORY CONTENTS
SORT FILES
SEARCH FOR FILES

COPY FILES
MOVE FILES
RENAME FILES
DELETE FILES

Sort Files by Size (smallest first)

C:\>DIR \DATA\WPDATA /OS_

1 Type **DIR** (for **DIR**ectory) and then press the **Spacebar**.

2 Type the path to the directory containing the files you want to sort (example: **\DATA\WPDATA**) and then press the **Spacebar**.

3 Type **/OS** (for **O**rder by **S**ize).

Note: To sort your files by size (largest first), type /O-S

Sort Files by Date (earliest first)

C:\>DIR \DOS /OD /P_

1 Type **DIR** (for **DIR**ectory) and then press the **Spacebar**.

2 Type the path to the directory containing the files you want to sort (example: **\DOS**) and then press the **Spacebar**.

3 Type **/OD** (for **O**rder by **D**ate).

Note: To sort your files by date (latest first), type /O-D

4 If you want to display the files one screen at a time, press the **Spacebar** and then type **/P** (for **P**ause).

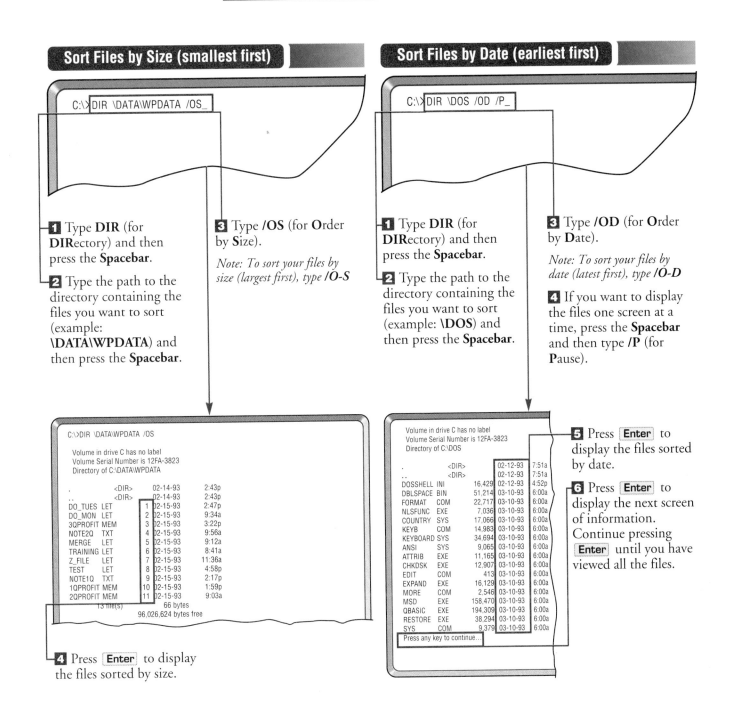

```
C:\>DIR \DATA\WPDATA /OS

 Volume in drive C has no label
 Volume Serial Number is 12FA-3823
 Directory of C:\DATA\WPDATA

.            <DIR>        02-14-93    2:43p
..           <DIR>        02-14-93    2:43p
DO_TUES  LET          1   02-15-93    2:47p
DO_MON   LET          2   02-15-93    9:34a
3QPROFIT MEM          3   02-15-93    3:22p
NOTE2Q   TXT          4   02-15-93    9:56a
MERGE    LET          5   02-15-93    9:12a
TRAINING LET          6   02-15-93    8:41a
Z_FILE   LET          7   02-15-93   11:36a
TEST     LET          8   02-15-93    4:58p
NOTE1Q   TXT          9   02-15-93    2:17p
1QPROFIT MEM         10   02-15-93    1:59p
2QPROFIT MEM         11   02-15-93    9:03a
        13 file(s)           66 bytes
                 96,026,624 bytes free
```

4 Press **Enter** to display the files sorted by size.

```
 Volume in drive C has no label
 Volume Serial Number is 12FA-3823
 Directory of C:\DOS

.            <DIR>        02-12-93    7:51a
..           <DIR>        02-12-93    7:51a
DOSSHELL INI     16,429   02-12-93    4:52p
DBLSPACE BIN     51,214   03-10-93    6:00a
FORMAT   COM     22,717   03-10-93    6:00a
NLSFUNC  EXE      7,036   03-10-93    6:00a
COUNTRY  SYS     17,066   03-10-93    6:00a
KEYB     COM     14,983   03-10-93    6:00a
KEYBOARD SYS     34,694   03-10-93    6:00a
ANSI     SYS      9,065   03-10-93    6:00a
ATTRIB   EXE     11,165   03-10-93    6:00a
CHKDSK   EXE     12,907   03-10-93    6:00a
EDIT     COM        413   03-10-93    6:00a
EXPAND   EXE     16,129   03-10-93    6:00a
MORE     COM      2,546   03-10-93    6:00a
MSD      EXE    158,470   03-10-93    6:00a
QBASIC   EXE    194,309   03-10-93    6:00a
RESTORE  EXE     38,294   03-10-93    6:00a
SYS      COM      9,379   03-10-93    6:00a
Press any key to continue...
```

5 Press **Enter** to display the files sorted by date.

6 Press **Enter** to display the next screen of information. Continue pressing **Enter** until you have viewed all the files.

SEARCH FOR FILES

The Search command helps you find files stored on a hard or floppy drive.

MS-DOS searches the current directory and all its subdirectories. If you want to search the entire drive, make the root directory the current directory.

```
C:\DATA\WPDATA>CD\

C:\>DIR JIM.WK1 /S
```

1 To change to the root directory, type **CD** and then press `Enter`.

2 Type **DIR** (for **DIR**ectory) and then press the **Spacebar**.

3 Type the name of the file you want to search for (example: **JIM.WK1**) and then press the **Spacebar**.

4 Type **/S** (for **S**earch) and then press `Enter`.

Search for Files Using Wildcards

Wildcards enable you to search for several files at the same time.

In this example, MS-DOS searches for all file names starting with PLAN, with any extension.

INTRODUCTION TO FILES
INTRODUCTION TO WILDCARDS
DIRECTORY CONTENTS
SORT FILES
SEARCH FOR FILES

COPY FILES
MOVE FILES
RENAME FILES
DELETE FILES

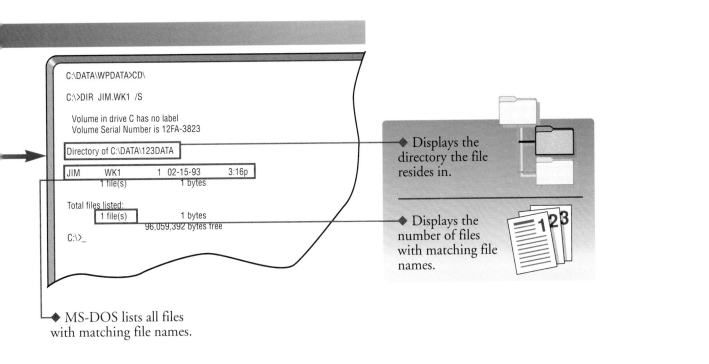

```
C:\DATA\WPDATA>CD\

C:\>DIR  JIM.WK1  /S

  Volume in drive C has no label
  Volume Serial Number is 12FA-3823

Directory of C:\DATA\123DATA

JIM     WK1      1  02-15-93      3:16p
          1 file(s)           1 bytes

Total files listed:
      1 file(s)            1 bytes
             96,059,392 bytes free

C:\>_
```

◆ Displays the directory the file resides in.

◆ Displays the number of files with matching file names.

◆ MS-DOS lists all files with matching file names.

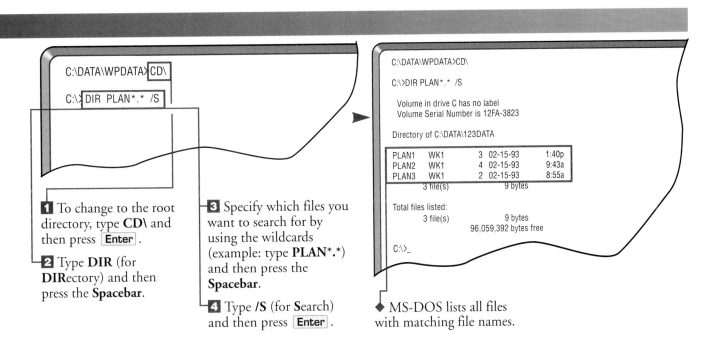

```
C:\DATA\WPDATA>CD\

C:\> DIR  PLAN*.*  /S
```

```
C:\DATA\WPDATA>CD\

C:\>DIR PLAN*.*  /S

  Volume in drive C has no label
  Volume Serial Number is 12FA-3823

Directory of C:\DATA\123DATA

PLAN1   WK1    3  02-15-93    1:40p
PLAN2   WK1    4  02-15-93    9:43a
PLAN3   WK1    2  02-15-93    8:55a
          3 file(s)         9 bytes

Total files listed:
      3 file(s)         9 bytes
             96,059,392 bytes free

C:\>_
```

1 To change to the root directory, type **CD** and then press **Enter**.

2 Type **DIR** (for **DIR**ectory) and then press the **Spacebar**.

3 Specify which files you want to search for by using the wildcards (example: type **PLAN*.***) and then press the **Spacebar**.

4 Type **/S** (for **S**earch) and then press **Enter**.

◆ MS-DOS lists all files with matching file names.

COPY FILES

The Copy command lets you make exact copies of your files and place them in a new location.

The original files remain unaffected.

The Copy command is:

| COPY | SOURCE | DESTINATION |

SOURCE	Tells MS-DOS the location (drive and directory) and name of the file(s) you want to copy.
DESTINATION	Tells MS-DOS where (drive and directory) you want to copy the file(s). This can also tell MS-DOS the new name for the file(s).

Note: If you omit the Source drive and directory, the file(s) in the current drive and directory is copied.

If you omit the Destination drive and directory, the file(s) is copied within the current drive and directory.

It is easier to type the COPY command if you first change to the directory that contains the file(s) you want to copy.

TO CHANGE THE CURRENT DIRECTORY

1 Type **CD** (for **C**hange **D**irectory) and then press the **Spacebar**.

2 Type the path to the directory you want to change to (example: **\DATA\WPDATA**) and then press Enter .

Copy Files within the Same Drive

COPY WITHIN THE SAME DIRECTORY

To copy a file within the same directory, you must change its name.

In this example, the MERGE.LET file is copied within the same directory and renamed MERGE.OLD.

```
C:\>CD \DATA\WPDATA

C:\DATA\WPDATA>COPY MERGE.LET MERGE.OLD
         1 file(s) copied

C:\DATA\WPDATA>_
```

1 Change to the directory that contains the file you want to copy.

2 Type **COPY** and then press the **Spacebar**.

3 Type the name of the file you want to copy (example: **MERGE.LET**) and then press the **Spacebar**.

4 Type a name for the new file (example: **MERGE.OLD**) and then press Enter .

COPY TO ANOTHER DIRECTORY

When copying a file to another directory, you can keep its name.

In this example, the MERGE.LET file is copied to the DATA directory.

COPY USING WILDCARDS

Wildcards enable you to copy several files at the same time.

In this example, all files with the MEM extension are copied to the DATA directory.

```
C:\>CD \DATA\WPDATA

C:\DATA\WPDATA>COPY MERGE.LET \DATA
            1 file(s) copied

C:\DATA\WPDATA>_
```

```
C:\>CD \DATA\WPDATA

C:\DATA\WPDATA>COPY *.MEM \DATA
1QPROFIT.MEM
2QPROFIT.MEM
3QPROFIT.MEM
            3 file(s) copied

C:\DATA\WPDATA>_
```

1 Change to the directory that contains the file you want to copy.

2 Type **COPY** and then press the **Spacebar**.

3 Type the name of the file you want to copy (example: **MERGE.LET**) and then press the **Spacebar**.

4 Type the path to the directory you want to copy the file to (example: **\DATA**) and then press Enter .

1 Change to the directory that contains the files you want to copy.

2 Type **COPY** and then press the **Spacebar**.

3 Specify which files you want to copy by using the wildcards (example: type ***.MEM**) and then press the **Spacebar**.

4 Type the path to the directory you want to copy the files to (example: **\DATA**) and then press Enter .

COPY FILES

Before copying files to a floppy drive, make sure you insert a formatted diskette into the drive.

COPY USING THE SAME NAME

In this example, the MERGE.LET file is copied to a diskette.

MERGE.LET

THE DRIVE NAME

B: = "B drive"

◆ The drive name consists of two parts: the letter and a colon (:). The colon represents the word "drive." For example, typing **B:** refers to the **B drive**.

```
C:\>CD \DATA\WPDATA

C:\DATA\WPDATA>COPY MERGE.LET B:\
        1 file(s) copied

C:\DATA\WPDATA>_
```

1 Change to the directory that contains the file you want to copy.

2 Type **COPY** and then press the **Spacebar**.

3 Type the name of the file you want to copy (example: **MERGE.LET**) and then press the **Spacebar**.

4 Type the drive name, then type the path to the directory you want to copy the file to (example: **B:**). Then press **Enter**.

Note: The \ stands for the root directory of the drive.

42

| GETTING STARTED | MANAGE DIRECTORIES | MANAGE FILES | MANAGE DISKETTES | MS-DOS SHELL | BACKUP | DATA PROTECTION | DISK MANAGEMENT |

INTRODUCTION TO FILES
INTRODUCTION TO WILDCARDS
DIRECTORY CONTENTS
SORT FILES
SEARCH FOR FILES

COPY FILES
MOVE FILES
RENAME FILES
DELETE FILES

COPY USING A DIFFERENT NAME

In this example, the MERGE.LET file is copied to a diskette and renamed MERGE.OLD.

COPY USING WILDCARDS

Wildcards enable you to copy several files at the same time. In this example, all files with the MEM extension are copied to a diskette.

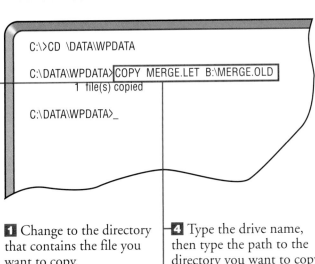

```
C:\>CD \DATA\WPDATA

C:\DATA\WPDATA>COPY MERGE.LET B:\MERGE.OLD
        1 file(s) copied

C:\DATA\WPDATA>_
```

```
C:\>CD \DATA\WPDATA

C:\DATA\WPDATA>COPY *.MEM B:\
1QPROFIT.MEM
2QPROFIT.MEM
3QPROFIT.MEM
        3 file(s) copied

C:\DATA\WPDATA>_
```

1 Change to the directory that contains the file you want to copy.

2 Type **COPY** and then press the **Spacebar**.

3 Type the name of the file you want to copy (example: **MERGE.LET**) and then press the **Spacebar**.

4 Type the drive name, then type the path to the directory you want to copy the file to (example: **B:**).

Note: The \ stands for the root directory of the drive.

5 Type a name for the new file (example: **MERGE.OLD**) and then press **Enter**.

1 Change to the directory that contains the files you want to copy.

2 Type **COPY** and then press the **Spacebar**.

3 Specify which files you want to copy by using the wildcards (example: type ***.MEM**) and then press the **Spacebar**.

4 Type the drive name, then type the path to the directory you want to copy the files to (example: **B:**). Then press **Enter**.

Note: The \ stands for the root directory of the drive.

MOVE FILES

The Move command lets you remove your files from one location and place them in another.

The Move command is:
MOVE · **SOURCE** · **DESTINATION**

SOURCE	Tells MS-DOS the location (drive and directory) and name of the file(s) you want to move.
DESTINATION	Tells MS-DOS where (drive and directory) you want to move the file(s). This can also tell MS-DOS the new name for the file(s).

Note: If you omit the Source drive and directory, the file(s) in the current drive and directory is moved.

If you omit the Destination drive, the file(s) is moved within the current drive.

It is easier to type the MOVE command if you first change to the directory that contains the file(s) you want to move.

MOVE TO A DIFFERENT DIRECTORY

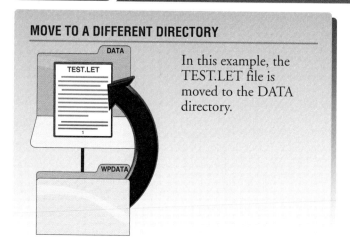

In this example, the TEST.LET file is moved to the DATA directory.

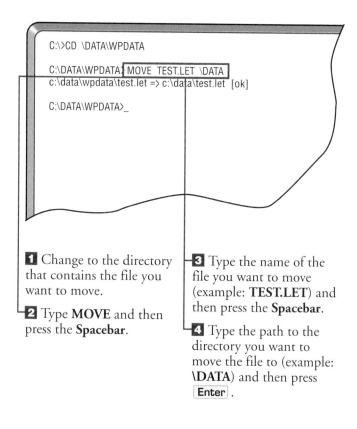

```
C:\>CD \DATA\WPDATA

C:\DATA\WPDATA> MOVE  TEST.LET  \DATA
c:\data\wpdata\test.let => c:\data\test.let  [ok]

C:\DATA\WPDATA>_
```

1 Change to the directory that contains the file you want to move.

2 Type **MOVE** and then press the **Spacebar**.

3 Type the name of the file you want to move (example: **TEST.LET**) and then press the **Spacebar**.

4 Type the path to the directory you want to move the file to (example: **\DATA**) and then press **Enter**.

GETTING STARTED	MANAGE DIRECTORIES	MANAGE FILES	MANAGE DISKETTES	MS-DOS SHELL	BACKUP	DATA PROTECTION	DISK MANAGEMENT

INTRODUCTION TO FILES   COPY FILES
INTRODUCTION TO WILDCARDS   **MOVE FILES**
DIRECTORY CONTENTS   RENAME FILES
SORT FILES   DELETE FILES
SEARCH FOR FILES

MOVE TO A DIFFERENT DRIVE

In this example, the TRAINING.LET file is moved to a diskette.

MOVE USING WILDCARDS

Wildcards enable you to move several files at the same time.

In this example, all files starting with NOTE, with the TXT extension, are moved to the DATA directory.

```
C:\>CD \DATA\WPDATA

C:\DATA\WPDATA>MOVE  TRAINING.LET  B:\
c:\data\wpdata\training.let => b:\training.let  [ok]

C:\DATA\WPDATA>_
```

```
C:\>CD  \DATA\WPDATA

C:\DATA\WPDATA>MOVE  NOTE*.TXT  \DATA
c:\data\wpdata\note1q.txt => c:\data\note1q.txt  [ok]
c:\data\wpdata\note2q.txt => c:\data\note2q.txt  [ok]

C:\DATA\WPDATA>_
```

1 Change to the directory that contains the file you want to move.

2 Type **MOVE** and then press the **Spacebar**.

3 Type the name of the file you want to move (example: **TRAINING.LET**) and then press the **Spacebar**.

4 Type the drive name, then type the path to the directory you want to move the file to (example: **B:**). Then press **Enter**.

Note: The \ stands for the root directory of the drive.

1 Change to the directory that contains the files you want to move.

2 Type **MOVE** and then press the **Spacebar**.

3 Specify which files you want to move by using the wildcards (example: type **NOTE*.TXT**) and then press the **Spacebar**.

4 Type the path to the directory you want to move the files to (example: **\DATA**) and then press **Enter**.

RENAME FILES

The Rename command lets you change the name of one or more files.

The Rename command is:

| RENAME | DRIVE | PATH | FILENAME1 | FILENAME2 |

DRIVE	Tells MS-DOS the drive containing the file(s) you want to rename.
PATH	Tells MS-DOS the path to the directory containing the file(s) you want to rename.
FILENAME1	Tells MS-DOS the name of the file(s) you want to rename.
FILENAME2	Tells MS-DOS the new name for the file(s).

Note: If you omit the drive and path, MS-DOS renames the file(s) in the current drive and directory.

It is easier to type the RENAME command if you first change to the directory that contains the file(s) you want to rename.

IMPORTANT!

Since every file in a directory must have a unique name, you cannot rename a file using a file name that already exists.

Rename a File

In this example, the DO_TUES.LET file is renamed DO_WED.TXT.

Rename Files Using Wildcards

Wildcards enable you to rename several files at the same time.

In this example, all files with the MEM extension are renamed with the OLD extension.

INTRODUCTION TO FILES
INTRODUCTION TO WILDCARDS
DIRECTORY CONTENTS
SORT FILES
SEARCH FOR FILES

COPY FILES
MOVE FILES
RENAME FILES
DELETE FILES

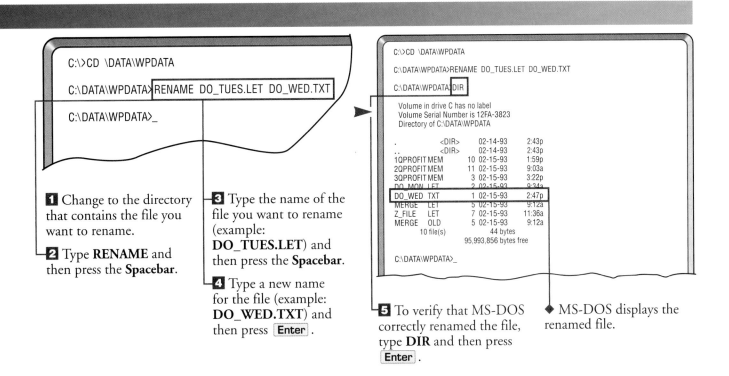

```
C:\>CD \DATA\WPDATA

C:\DATA\WPDATA>RENAME DO_TUES.LET DO_WED.TXT

C:\DATA\WPDATA>_
```

1 Change to the directory that contains the file you want to rename.

2 Type **RENAME** and then press the **Spacebar**.

3 Type the name of the file you want to rename (example: **DO_TUES.LET**) and then press the **Spacebar**.

4 Type a new name for the file (example: **DO_WED.TXT**) and then press **Enter**.

```
C:\>CD \DATA\WPDATA

C:\DATA\WPDATA>RENAME DO_TUES.LET DO_WED.TXT

C:\DATA\WPDATA>DIR

    Volume in drive C has no label
    Volume Serial Number is 12FA-3823
    Directory of C:\DATA\WPDATA

.              <DIR>        02-14-93      2:43p
..             <DIR>        02-14-93      2:43p
1QPROFIT MEM      10 02-15-93      1:59p
2QPROFIT MEM      11 02-15-93      9:03a
3QPROFIT MEM       3 02-15-93      3:22p
DO_MON  LET        2 02-15-93      9:34a
DO_WED  TXT        1 02-15-93      2:47p
MERGE   LET        5 02-15-93      9:12a
Z_FILE  LET        7 02-15-93     11:36a
MERGE   OLD        5 02-15-93      9:12a
      10 file(s)          44 bytes
                  95,993,856 bytes free

C:\DATA\WPDATA>_
```

5 To verify that MS-DOS correctly renamed the file, type **DIR** and then press **Enter**.

◆ MS-DOS displays the renamed file.

```
C:\>CD \DATA\WPDATA

C:\DATA\WPDATA>RENAME *.MEM *.OLD

C:\DATA\WPDATA>_
```

1 Change to the directory that contains the files you want to rename.

2 Type **RENAME** and then press the **Spacebar**.

3 Specify which files you want to rename by using the wildcards (example: type *.**MEM**) and then press the **Spacebar**.

4 Specify a new name for the files by using the wildcards (example: type *.**OLD**) and then press **Enter**.

DELETE FILES

The Delete command (typed as DEL) lets you erase files that you no longer require.

The Delete command is:

DEL	DRIVE	PATH	FILENAME	/P

DEL	Stands for DELete.
DRIVE	Tells MS-DOS the drive containing the file(s) you want to delete.
PATH	Tells MS-DOS the path to the directory containing the file(s) you want to delete.
FILENAME	Tells MS-DOS the name of the file(s) you want to delete.
/P	Tells MS-DOS to ask you for confirmation before deleting a file.

Note: If you omit the drive and path, MS-DOS deletes the file(s) in the current drive and directory.

It is easier to type the DELETE command if you first change to the directory that contains the file(s) you want to delete.

You can use Delete Sentry to fully recover deleted files. For more information, refer to page 98.

Delete a File

In this example, the DO_MON.LET file is deleted.

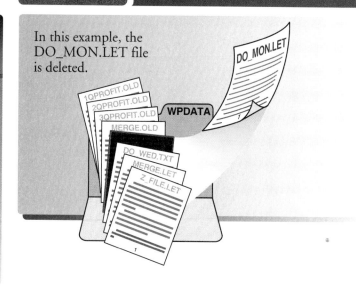

Delete Files Using Wildcards

Wildcards enable you to delete several files at the same time.

In this example, all files with the OLD extension are deleted.

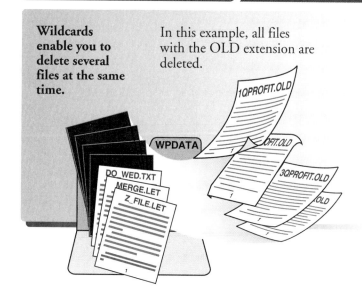

INTRODUCTION TO FILES   COPY FILES
INTRODUCTION TO WILDCARDS   MOVE FILES
DIRECTORY CONTENTS   RENAME FILES
SORT FILES   **DELETE FILES**
SEARCH FOR FILES

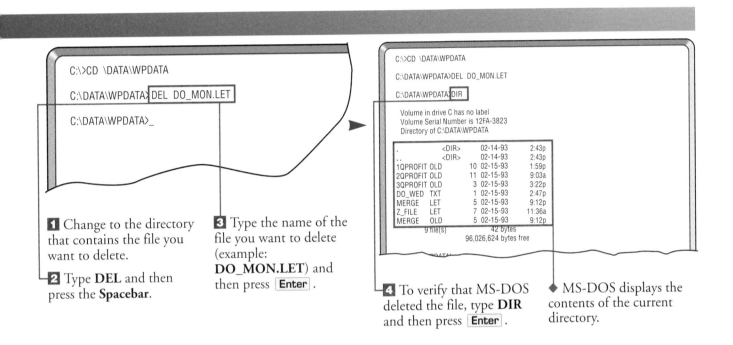

1 Change to the directory that contains the file you want to delete.

2 Type **DEL** and then press the **Spacebar**.

3 Type the name of the file you want to delete (example: **DO_MON.LET**) and then press **Enter**.

4 To verify that MS-DOS deleted the file, type **DIR** and then press **Enter**.

◆ MS-DOS displays the contents of the current directory.

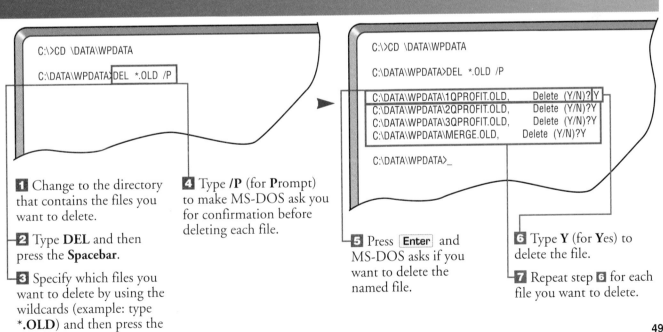

1 Change to the directory that contains the files you want to delete.

2 Type **DEL** and then press the **Spacebar**.

3 Specify which files you want to delete by using the wildcards (example: type *.**OLD**) and then press the **Spacebar**.

4 Type **/P** (for **P**rompt) to make MS-DOS ask you for confirmation before deleting each file.

5 Press **Enter** and MS-DOS asks if you want to delete the named file.

6 Type **Y** (for **Y**es) to delete the file.

7 Repeat step **6** for each file you want to delete.

INTRODUCTION TO DISKETTES

Diskettes

You can store programs and data on diskettes (or floppy disks). Diskettes are commonly used to transfer information from one computer to another or to make a backup copy of a hard drive's contents.

5.25" DISKETTE

◆ Most diskettes have a label to describe their contents. Use a soft-tipped felt marker to write on the label. A pen or pencil may damage the diskette.

◆ You can "write-protect" a diskette to prevent erasing or recording information on it. To write-protect a 5.25" diskette, place a small sticker over the notch on the diskette.

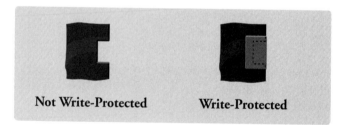

Not Write-Protected   **Write-Protected**

3.5" DISKETTE

MicroFLOPPY
Double Sided

◆ A 3.5" diskette has a write-protect tab. You can only record and erase data on the diskette when the tab is in the "Not Write-Protected" position.

Not Write-Protected   **Write-Protected**

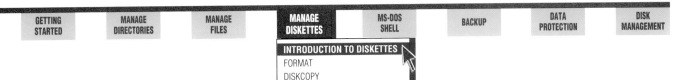

| GETTING STARTED | MANAGE DIRECTORIES | MANAGE FILES | MANAGE DISKETTES | MS-DOS SHELL | BACKUP | DATA PROTECTION | DISK MANAGEMENT |

INTRODUCTION TO DISKETTES
FORMAT
DISKCOPY

Diskette Capacity

The capacity of a diskette tells you how much information a diskette can store.

If a typed page contains 1,000 characters (approximately 1K), then a 720K diskette can store 720 pages of information.

Note: 1,000K equals 1MB.

720 PAGES

1 PAGE

1K   **720K**

5.25 and 3.5 inch diskettes offer two types of storage capacities.

◆ A "high-density" diskette can store more information than a "double-density" diskette of the same size.

	Capacity	
Type	5.25"	3.5"
Double-Density (DD)	360K	720K
High-Density (HD)	1.2MB	1.44MB

Floppy Drives

Floppy drives store programs and data onto diskettes.

5.25" FLOPPY DRIVE

This drive works with 5.25" diskettes.

◆ When your computer accesses the floppy drive, a light on the front of the drive turns on.

◆ This drive uses a door latch to secure a diskette. You can insert or remove a diskette when the door latch is in the "up" position.

3.5" FLOPPY DRIVE

This drive works with 3.5" diskettes.

◆ When your computer accesses the floppy drive, a light on the front of the drive turns on.

◆ To insert a diskette, push it gently into the floppy drive. To remove the diskette, press the "eject" button.

This chart shows the types of diskettes you can use with double-density and high-density drives.

	Type of Diskette			
Type of Drive	Double-Density	High-Density	Double-Density	High-Density
Double-Density	●		●	
High-Density	●	●	◐	●

● A high-density drive can read a 5.25" double-density diskette, but should not be used to write to it.

FORMAT

Format a Diskette

You must format a diskette before storing data on it. Formatting prepares the diskette for use.

```
C:\>FORMAT B:
Insert new diskette for drive B:
and press ENTER when ready... _
```

1 Type **FORMAT** and then press the **Spacebar**.

2 Type the name of the drive that contains the diskette you want to format (example: **B:**) and then press `Enter`.

3 Insert the diskette into the drive and then press `Enter`.

The Format command is:

FORMAT | DRIVE

DRIVE   Tells MS-DOS which drive contains the diskette you want to format.

THE DRIVE NAME

B: = **"B drive"**   To indicate which drive contains the diskette you want to format, type a colon (**:**) after the drive letter. The colon represents the word "drive." For example, typing **B:** refers to the **B drive**.

◆ The Format command erases all the information on a diskette. Do not format a diskette containing information you want to retain.

◆ If you accidentally format a diskette, it may be possible to recover all of its files by using the Unformat command. Refer to your Microsoft User's Guide or check with a computer expert.

CAUTION

INTRODUCTION TO DISKETTES
FORMAT
DISKCOPY

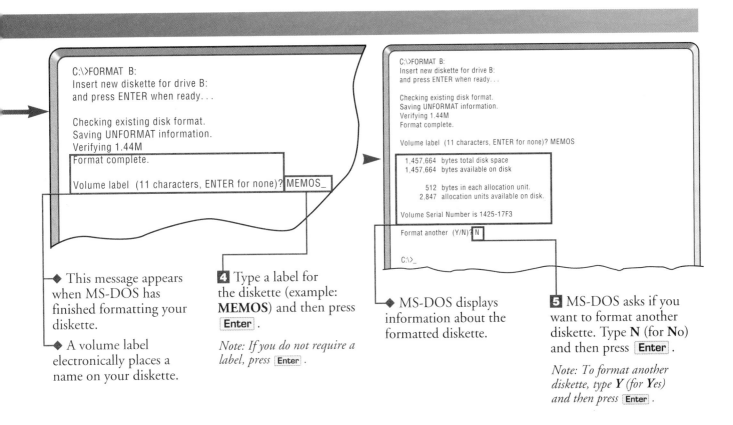

```
C:\>FORMAT B:
Insert new diskette for drive B:
and press ENTER when ready...

Checking existing disk format.
Saving UNFORMAT information.
Verifying 1.44M
Format complete.

Volume label  (11 characters, ENTER for none)? MEMOS_
```

```
C:\>FORMAT B:
Insert new diskette for drive B:
and press ENTER when ready...

Checking existing disk format.
Saving UNFORMAT information.
Verifying 1.44M
Format complete.

Volume label  (11 characters, ENTER for none)? MEMOS

1,457,664  bytes total disk space
1,457,664  bytes available on disk

     512  bytes in each allocation unit.
   2,847  allocation units available on disk.

Volume Serial Number is 1425-17F3

Format another  (Y/N)? N

C:\>_
```

◆ This message appears when MS-DOS has finished formatting your diskette.

◆ A volume label electronically places a name on your diskette.

4 Type a label for the diskette (example: **MEMOS**) and then press **Enter**.

Note: If you do not require a label, press **Enter**.

◆ MS-DOS displays information about the formatted diskette.

5 MS-DOS asks if you want to format another diskette. Type **N** (for **N**o) and then press **Enter**.

*Note: To format another diskette, type **Y** (for **Y**es) and then press* **Enter**.

Display a Volume Label

You can display the volume label of a diskette, if it has one.

Note: You can label a diskette during the Format process.

Letters

Memos

MicroFLOPPY
Double Sided

```
C:\>VOL B:

Volume in drive B is MEMOS
Volume Serial Number is 1425-17F3

C:\>_
```

1 Type **VOL** and then press the **Spacebar**.

2 Type the name of the drive that contains the diskette whose volume label you want to display (example: **B:**).

3 Press **Enter** and the volume label appears.

DISKCOPY

The Diskcopy command lets you copy the entire contents of one diskette to another. The second diskette becomes an exact copy of the first one.

SOURCE DISKETTE

Copy a Disk

The Diskcopy command is:

DISKCOPY	SOURCE	TARGET

SOURCE — Tells MS-DOS which drive you want to copy the files from.

TARGET — Tells MS-DOS which drive you want to copy the files to.

```
C:\> DISKCOPY B: B:

Insert SOURCE diskette in drive B:

Press any key to continue . . .
_
```

1 Type **DISKCOPY** and then press the **Spacebar**.

2 Type the name of the drive you want to copy the files **from** (example: **B:**) and then press the **Spacebar**.

3 Type the name of the drive you want to copy the files **to** (example: **B:**) and then press Enter .

4 Insert the **SOURCE** diskette into the drive and then press Enter .

INTRODUCTION TO DISKETTES
FORMAT
DISKCOPY

Note: The source and target diskettes must be the same size and capacity.

TARGET DISKETTE

The Diskcopy command automatically formats the target diskette during the copy process. Its contents are completely destroyed, so make sure it does not contain any files you want to keep.

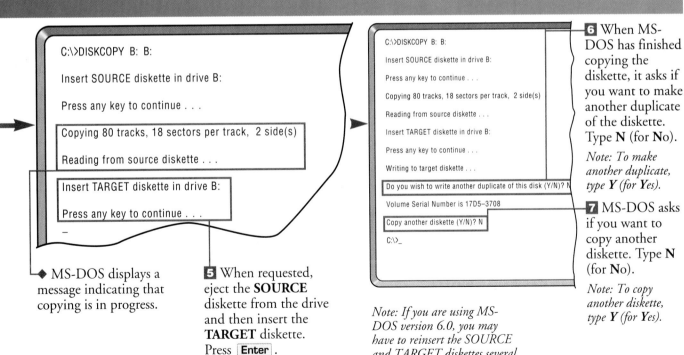

```
C:\>DISKCOPY B:  B:

Insert SOURCE diskette in drive B:

Press any key to continue . . .

Copying 80 tracks, 18 sectors per track,  2 side(s)

Reading from source diskette . . .

Insert TARGET diskette in drive B:

Press any key to continue . . .

_
```

◆ MS-DOS displays a message indicating that copying is in progress.

5 When requested, eject the **SOURCE** diskette from the drive and then insert the **TARGET** diskette. Press **Enter**.

```
C:\>DISKCOPY B:  B:

Insert SOURCE diskette in drive B:

Press any key to continue . . .

Copying 80 tracks, 18 sectors per track,  2 side(s)

Reading from source diskette . . .

Insert TARGET diskette in drive B:

Press any key to continue . . .

Writing to target diskette . . .

Do you wish to write another duplicate of this disk (Y/N)? N

Volume Serial Number is 17D5-3708

Copy another diskette (Y/N)? N

C:\>_
```

Note: If you are using MS-DOS version 6.0, you may have to reinsert the SOURCE and TARGET diskettes several times.

6 When MS-DOS has finished copying the diskette, it asks if you want to make another duplicate of the diskette. Type **N** (for **N**o).

*Note: To make another duplicate, type **Y** (for **Y**es).*

7 MS-DOS asks if you want to copy another diskette. Type **N** (for **N**o).

*Note: To copy another diskette, type **Y** (for **Y**es).*

START THE MS-DOS SHELL

1 To start the MS-DOS Shell, type **DOSSHELL** and then press `Enter`.

`C:\>DOSSHELL_`

KEY COMBINATIONS

◆ If key names are separated by a plus (+) sign, press and hold down the first key before pressing the second key (example: `Shift` + `Tab`).

◆ If key names are separated by a comma (,), press and release the first key before pressing the second key (example: `Alt`, `F`).

POWER
TURBO
H/DRIVE

TURBO   RESET

AD2

Num Lock   Caps Lock   Scroll Lock

| GETTING STARTED | MANAGE DIRECTORIES | MANAGE FILES | MANAGE DISKETTES | MS-DOS SHELL | BACKUP | DATA PROTECTION | DISK MANAGEMENT |

GETTING STARTED ▶   START THE MS-DOS SHELL
MANAGE DIRECTORIES ▶   MOUSE BASICS
MANAGE FILES ▶   SELECT COMMANDS
                           CHANGE SCREEN DISPLAY AND COLORS
                           HELP

The MS-DOS Shell

The **Drive** area displays the drives in your computer. The current drive is highlighted (example: drive **C**).

The **Directory Tree** area displays the directories in the current drive. The current directory is highlighted (example: **C:**).

The MS-DOS Shell provides an easy, graphic approach to using most commands.

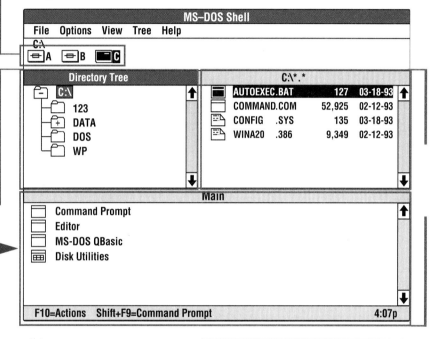

The **File** area lists all the files in the current directory.

The **Main** area lists the programs and utilities installed in your computer.

If the **Main** area is not displayed, press `Alt`, `V`, `F` to display it.

Note: If the graphics in the above screen do not match your display, refer to "Change Screen Display and Colors" on page 62.

SELECT AN AREA

◆ To move from one area to another, press `Tab`. The MS-DOS Shell highlights the bar above the selected area.

◆ To move in the opposite direction, press `Shift` + `Tab`.

 Using the Mouse

● Move the pointer � anywhere in the area you want to select and then click the left mouse button.

MOUSE
BASICS

Using a Mouse

With MS-DOS, you can use a mouse to replace hard-to-remember key combinations with easy "point and click" actions.

◆ You can use the mouse buttons to:

●◦ start programs

●◦ select commands

●◦ choose options

◆ Under the mouse is a ball which senses the movement of the mouse. You should remove and clean this ball occasionally.

Holding the Mouse

Hold the mouse as shown in the diagram. This way, your thumb and two rightmost fingers guide the mouse while your two remaining fingers press the mouse buttons.

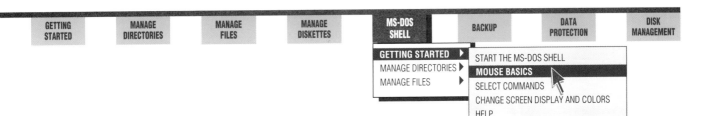

GETTING STARTED ▶
MANAGE DIRECTORIES ▶
MANAGE FILES ▶

START THE MS-DOS SHELL
MOUSE BASICS
SELECT COMMANDS
CHANGE SCREEN DISPLAY AND COLORS
HELP

Moving the Mouse Pointer

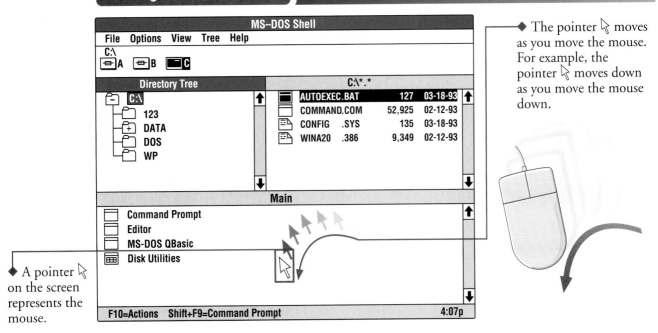

◆ The pointer ⬉ moves as you move the mouse. For example, the pointer ⬉ moves down as you move the mouse down.

◆ A pointer ⬉ on the screen represents the mouse.

Common Mouse Terms

TERM	WHAT IT MEANS
Point	Move the pointer ⬉ on the screen until it is over the desired location.
Click	Quickly press and release the left mouse button.
Double-Click	Quickly press and release the left mouse button twice.
Drag	Hold down the left mouse button while moving the mouse.
Drag and Drop	Hold down the left mouse button while moving the mouse. Release the mouse button when the pointer ⬉ is over the desired location.

59

SELECT COMMANDS

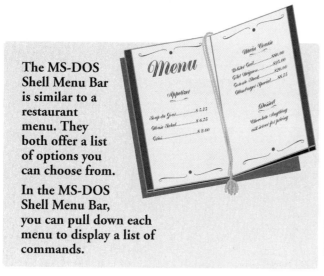

The MS-DOS Shell Menu Bar is similar to a restaurant menu. They both offer a list of options you can choose from.

In the MS-DOS Shell Menu Bar, you can pull down each menu to display a list of commands.

1 Press **Alt** to activate the **Menu Bar**.

◆ The **File** menu name is highlighted.

Using the Mouse

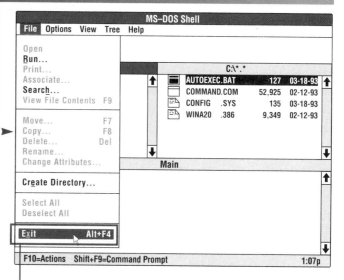

1 To open a menu, click the menu name (example: **File**).

● The **File** menu appears.

2 To select a command, click the command name (example: **Exit**).

TO CLOSE A MENU

Click anywhere outside the menu area.

60

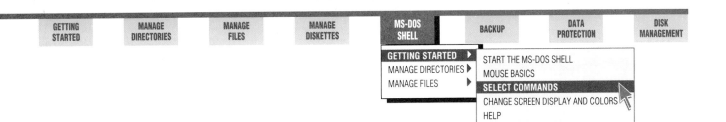

| GETTING STARTED | MANAGE DIRECTORIES | MANAGE FILES | MANAGE DISKETTES | MS-DOS SHELL | BACKUP | DATA PROTECTION | DISK MANAGEMENT |

GETTING STARTED ▶
MANAGE DIRECTORIES ▶
MANAGE FILES ▶

START THE MS-DOS SHELL
MOUSE BASICS
SELECT COMMANDS
CHANGE SCREEN DISPLAY AND COLORS
HELP

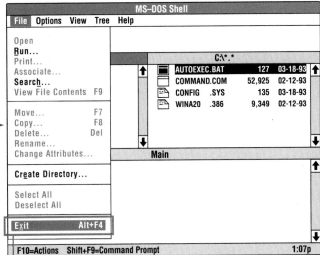

2 To open a menu, press the underlined letter in the menu name (example: **F** for **F**ile).

or

Press **→** until you highlight the menu name and then press **Enter** .

◆ The **File** menu appears.

TO CLOSE A MENU

Press **Esc** .

3 To select a command, press the underlined letter in the command name (example: **X** for E**x**it).

or

Press **↓** until you highlight the command name and then press **Enter** .

*Note: To restart the MS-DOS Shell, type **DOSSHELL** and then press* **Enter** .

CHANGE SCREEN DISPLAY AND COLORS

Change Screen Display

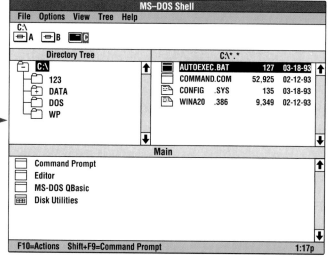

When you first start the MS-DOS Shell, the above screen appears.

If your computer has color graphics capability, you can change its screen display and colors.

1 Press `Alt`, `O`, `D` and the **Screen Display Mode** dialog box appears.

2 Press `↓` or `↑` until you highlight the desired screen display mode and then press `Enter`.

◆ The new screen display mode appears (example: **Graphics 25 lines Low Resolution**).

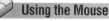 **Using the Mouse**

❶ Click **Options** to open its menu.

❷ Click **Display** and the **Screen Display Mode** dialog box appears.

❸ Click the desired screen display mode.

❹ Click the **OK** button.

GETTING STARTED ▶
MANAGE DIRECTORIES ▶
MANAGE FILES ▶

START THE MS-DOS SHELL
MOUSE BASICS
SELECT COMMANDS
CHANGE SCREEN DISPLAY AND COLORS
HELP

Change Screen Colors

1 Press Alt, O, O and the **Color Scheme** dialog box appears.

2 Press ↓ or ↑ until you highlight the desired color scheme and then press Enter.

◆ The new color scheme appears (example: **Basic Blue**).

Using the Mouse

❶ Click **Options** to open its menu.

❷ Click **Colors** and the **Color Scheme** dialog box appears.

❸ Click the desired color scheme.

❹ Click the **OK** button.

The MS-DOS Shell offers a variety of screen colors. Some examples are:

Hot Pink

Ocean

Emerald City

Turquoise

HELP

Getting Help on Commands and Procedures

Help information is available for all commands listed in each menu.

1 Press Alt to activate the **Menu Bar**.

2 To open a menu, press the underlined letter in the menu name (example: V for View).

3 Press ↓ until you highlight the command you want help on (example: **Dual File Lists**).

4 Press F1 and help information appears.

5 To display help information on a highlighted procedure (example: **Displaying Two File Lists**), press Enter.

Note: Some Help screens display more than one related procedure. To receive help on another procedure, press Tab until you highlight it and then press Enter.

TO CANCEL HELP

Press Esc.

Using the Mouse

1 To open a menu, click the menu name (example: **View**).

2 Press ↓ until you highlight the command you want help on (example: **Dual File Lists**).

3 Press F1 and help information appears.

4 Double-click a related procedure you want to display help information on (example: **Displaying Two File Lists**).

TO CANCEL HELP

Click Close.

GETTING STARTED ▶
MANAGE DIRECTORIES ▶
MANAGE FILES ▶

START THE MS-DOS SHELL
MOUSE BASICS
SELECT COMMANDS
CHANGE SCREEN DISPLAY AND COLORS
HELP

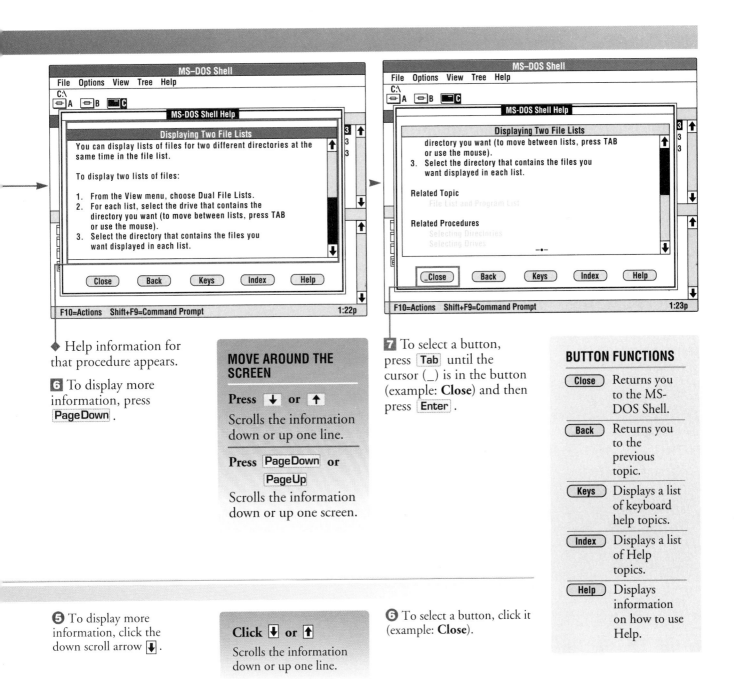

◆ Help information for that procedure appears.

6 To display more information, press **PageDown**.

MOVE AROUND THE SCREEN

Press ↓ or ↑
Scrolls the information down or up one line.

Press PageDown or PageUp
Scrolls the information down or up one screen.

7 To select a button, press **Tab** until the cursor (_) is in the button (example: **Close**) and then press **Enter**.

BUTTON FUNCTIONS

Close	Returns you to the MS-DOS Shell.
Back	Returns you to the previous topic.
Keys	Displays a list of keyboard help topics.
Index	Displays a list of Help topics.
Help	Displays information on how to use Help.

❺ To display more information, click the down scroll arrow ↓.

Click ↓ or ↑
Scrolls the information down or up one line.

❻ To select a button, click it (example: **Close**).

65

Change Drives

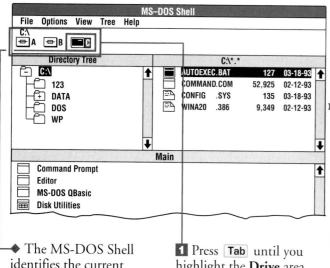

◆ The MS-DOS Shell identifies the current drive by highlighting its name (example: ☐C).

1 Press **Tab** until you highlight the **Drive** area.

2 Press **←** or **→** until you highlight the drive you want to change to (example: ☐A).

3 Press **Enter** and the **Directory Tree** area displays the directories in the new current drive.

Note: In this example, the diskette in drive A does not contain any files in the current directory.

Using the Mouse

❶ To change to another drive, click its icon (example: ☐A).

Note: To change back to drive C, click ☐C.

Before changing to a floppy drive, make sure you insert a diskette into the drive.

Shortcut for Steps 1 to 3

To change to drive **A**, press **Ctrl** + **A**.

To change to drive **B**, press **Ctrl** + **B**.

To change to drive **C**, press **Ctrl** + **C**.

Change Directories

◆ The MS-DOS Shell identifies the current directory by highlighting its name (example: **C:**).

1 Press **Tab** until you highlight the **Directory Tree** area.

2 To change to another directory, press **↓** or **↑** until you highlight the directory name (example: **DOS**).

◆ The **File** area displays the files in the new current directory.

Move within the Directory Tree Area

Press	Resulting Action
↑ or **↓**	Move up or down one directory
Home	Move to the root directory
End	Move to the last directory
Type the first letter of the directory name	Move to the directory starting with that letter

Using the Mouse

1 Click the name of the directory you want to change to (example: **DOS**).

Expand One Directory

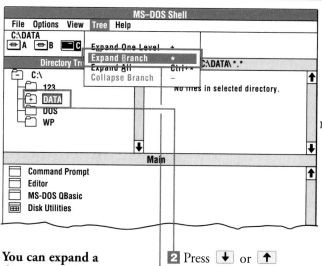

You can expand a directory to display its subdirectories.

Note: The plus (+) sign in a directory folder indicates that its subdirectories are hidden.

1 Press **Tab** until you highlight the **Directory Tree** area.

2 Press ↓ or ↑ until you highlight the directory you want to expand (example: **DATA**).

3 Press **Alt**, **T**, **B** to select the **Expand Branch** command.

Using the Mouse

❶ Click the name of the directory you want to expand (example: **DATA**).

❷ Click **Tree** to open its menu.

❸ Click **Expand Branch**.

◆ The current directory displays its subdirectories.

◆ A minus (–) sign appears in the folder.

Shortcut for Step 3

Press * (asterisk).

EXPAND ALL DIRECTORIES

1 Press **Tab** until you highlight the **Directory Tree** area.

2 Press **Alt**, **T**, **A** to select the **Expand All** command.

Using the Mouse

❶ Click **Tree** to open its menu.

❷ Click **Expand All**.

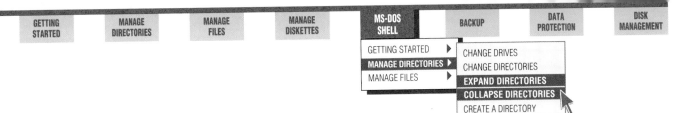

GETTING STARTED ▸
MANAGE DIRECTORIES ▸
MANAGE FILES ▸

CHANGE DRIVES
CHANGE DIRECTORIES
EXPAND DIRECTORIES
COLLAPSE DIRECTORIES
CREATE A DIRECTORY

Collapse One Directory

You can collapse a directory to hide its subdirectories.

Note: The minus (–) sign in a directory folder indicates that its subdirectories are displayed.

1 Press `Tab` until you highlight the **Directory Tree** area.

2 Press `↓` or `↑` until you highlight the directory you want to collapse (example: **DATA**).

3 Press `Alt`, `T`, `C` to select the **Collapse Branch** command.

Using the Mouse

❶ Click 🗁 beside the directory you want to collapse (example: **DATA**).

◆ The current directory hides its subdirectories.

◆ A plus (+) sign appears in the folder.

Shortcut for Step 3

Press `–` (minus sign).

COLLAPSE ALL DIRECTORIES

1 Press `Tab` until you highlight the **Directory Tree** area.

2 Press `↑` until you highlight the root directory (**C:**).

3 Press `Alt`, `T`, `C` to select the **Collapse Branch** command.

Using the Mouse

❶ Click 🗁 beside the root directory (**C:**).

CREATE A DIRECTORY

Create a Directory

1 Press **Tab** until you highlight the **Directory Tree** area.

2 Press **↓** or **↑** until you highlight the directory you want to contain the new directory (example: **C:**).

3 Press **Alt**, **F**, **E** to select the **Create Directory** command.

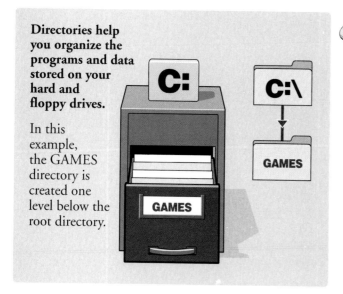

Directories help you organize the programs and data stored on your hard and floppy drives.

In this example, the GAMES directory is created one level below the root directory.

Using the Mouse

1 Click the directory you want to contain the new directory (example: **C:**).

2 Click **File** to open its menu.

3 Click **Create Directory**.

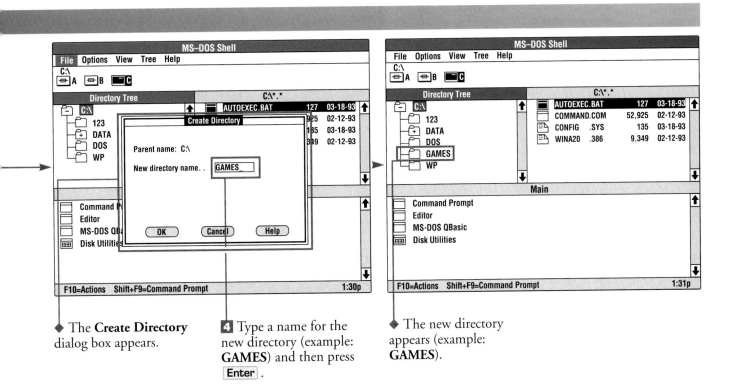

◆ The **Create Directory** dialog box appears.

4 Type a name for the new directory (example: **GAMES**) and then press Enter .

◆ The new directory appears (example: **GAMES**).

---

4 Type a name for the new directory (example: **GAMES**).

5 Click the **OK** button.

DELETE A DIRECTORY

1 Press Tab until you highlight the **Directory Tree** area.

2 Press ↓ or ↑ until you highlight the directory you want to delete.

3 Press Alt , F , D to select the **Delete** command.

4 Press Enter .

Using the Mouse

1 Click the directory you want to delete.

2 Click **File** to open its menu.

3 Click **Delete**.

4 Click the **Yes** button.

Note: You cannot delete a directory that contains subdirectories or files.

You can hide
the Main area
to increase the
Directory Tree
and File
display areas.

1 Press **Alt**, **V**, **S** to select the **Single File List** command.

Using the Mouse

1 Click **View** to open its menu.

2 Click **Single File List**.

(screen text)

MS-DOS Shell

File Options View Tree Help

C:\
A   B

		C:*.*		
Single File List		AUTOEXEC.BAT	127	03-18-93
Dual File Lists		COMMAND.COM	52,925	02-12-93
All Files		CONFIG .SYS	135	03-18-93
Program/File Lists		WINA20 .386	9,349	02-12-93
Program List				

Direct

123
DATA
1
W
DOS
WP

Repaint Screen   Shift+F5
Refresh   F5

Main

Command Prompt
Editor
MS-DOS QBasic
Disk Utilities

Main area

F10=Actions   Shift+F9=Command Prompt   3:00p

Single File List

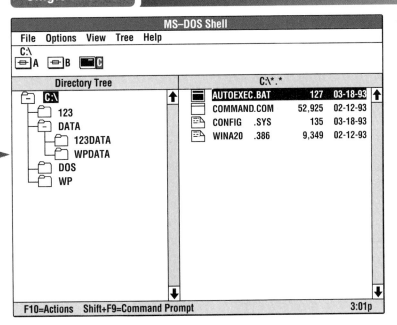

◆ The MS-DOS Shell changes to the **Single File List** view.

PROGRAM/FILE LISTS

To return to the Program/File Lists view:

1 Press `Alt`, `V`, `F` to select the **Program/File Lists** command.

Using the Mouse

1 Click **View** to open its menu.

2 Click **Program/File Lists**.

Select One File

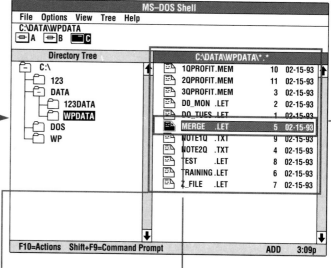

1 Press `Tab` until you highlight the **Directory Tree** area.

2 Press ↓ or ↑ until you highlight the directory that contains the file you want to select (example: **WPDATA**).

◆ The files in the highlighted directory appear.

3 Press `Tab` until you highlight the **File** area.

4 Press ↓ or ↑ until you highlight the file you want to select (example: **MERGE.LET**).

You must select a file before telling the MS-DOS Shell what to do with it.

Using the Mouse

1 Click the directory that contains the file you want to select (example: **WPDATA**).

2 Click the file you want to select (example: **MERGE.LET**).

GETTING STARTED ▶
MANAGE DIRECTORIES ▶
MANAGE FILES ▶

CHANGE VIEW
SELECT FILES
SEARCH FOR FILES
SORT FILES
COPY FILES
RENAME A FILE
DELETE FILES

Select Multiple Files

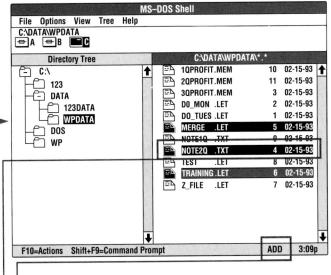

5 To select another file, press **Shift** + **F8** and the word **ADD** appears at the bottom of the screen.

6 Press **↓** or **↑** until you highlight the next file (example: **NOTE2Q.TXT**). Press the **Spacebar** to select it.

*Note: To deselect the file, press the **Spacebar** again.*

7 Repeat step **6** for each file you want to select.

8 Press **Shift** + **F8** to end the selection. The word **ADD** disappears.

❸ Hold down **Ctrl** as you click the other files you want to select.

Select All Files

1 Press **Alt**, **F**, **S** to select all files in the highlighted directory.

Shortcut

Press **Ctrl** + **/** (slash).

Using the Mouse

❶ Click **File** to open its menu.

❷ Click **Select All**.

DESELECT ALL FILES

1 To deselect all files, press **↓**.

Using the Mouse

❶ To deselect all files, click any file.

SEARCH
FOR FILES

Search for Files

You can use the MS-DOS Shell to search for a file or group of files.

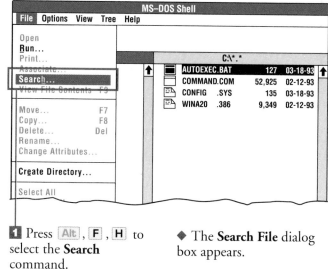

MS-DOS Shell

| File | Options | View | Tree | Help |

Open
Run...
Print...
Associate...
Search...
View File Contents F9

Move...   F7
Copy...   F8
Delete...   Del
Rename...
Change Attributes...

Create Directory...

Select All

C:*.*

AUTOEXEC.BAT	127	03-18-93
COMMAND.COM	52,925	02-12-93
CONFIG .SYS	135	03-18-93
WINA20 .386	9,349	02-12-93

1 Press <kbd>Alt</kbd>, <kbd>F</kbd>, <kbd>H</kbd> to select the **Search** command.

◆ The **Search File** dialog box appears.

 Using the Mouse

❶ Click **File** to open its menu.

❷ Click **Search** and the **Search File** dialog box appears.

2 Specify which files you want to search for by using the wildcards (example: type *.**WK1**).

*Note: To search for a specific file, type its file name (example: **PLAN1.WK1**).*

◆ In this example, the MS-DOS Shell will search for all file names with the **WK1** extension.

3 Press **Enter** to start the search.

◆ The MS-DOS Shell lists all matching files.

4 Press **Esc** to close the **Search Results** screen.

You can move, copy, delete or rename the files listed in the **Search Results** screen.

❸ Specify which files you want to search for by using the wildcards (example: type *.**WK1**).

*Note: To search for a specific file, type its file name (example: **PLAN1.WK1**).*

❹ Click the **OK** button to start the search.

Wildcards let you search for several files at the same time.

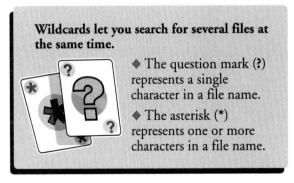

◆ The question mark (**?**) represents a single character in a file name.

◆ The asterisk (*) represents one or more characters in a file name.

Sort Files

1 Press **Tab** until you highlight the **Directory Tree** area.

2 Press **↓** or **↑** until you highlight the directory that contains the files you want to sort (example: **WPDATA**).

◆ The files in the highlighted directory appear.

3 Press **Alt**, **O**, **F** to select the **File Display Options** command.

Using the Mouse

1 Click the directory that contains the files you want to sort (example: **WPDATA**).

2 Click **Options** to open its menu.

3 Click **File Display Options** and its dialog box appears.

◆ The **File Display Options** dialog box appears.

4 Press **Tab** three times to move to the **Sort by:** options.

5 Press **↓** until you select the desired sort type (example: **Extension**) and ○ becomes ●. Then press **Enter**.

◆ The files are sorted (example: by extension).

4 Click the circle beside the desired sort type (example: **Extension**) and ○ becomes ●.

5 Click the **OK** button.

You can sort files by name, extension, date or size.

Name of the file

Date the file was created or last modified

File extension

Size of the file

The MS-DOS Shell lets you make an exact copy of a file and place it in a new location. The original file remains unaffected.

In this example, the TRAINING.LET file is copied to a diskette in drive A.

TRAINING.LET

Note: Before copying files to a floppy drive, make sure you insert a diskette into the drive.

Copy Files

1 Press `Tab` until you highlight the **Directory Tree** area.

2 Press ↓ or ↑ until you highlight the directory that contains the file you want to copy (example: **WPDATA**).

◆ The files in the highlighted directory appear.

Using the Mouse

1 Click the directory that contains the file you want to copy (example: **WPDATA**).

2 Click the file you want to copy (example: **TRAINING.LET**).

*Note: To copy more than one file, select them in step **2**. To select multiple files, refer to page 74.*

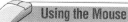

3 Press and hold down `Ctrl` as you drag the file to the drive (▱) or directory (🗁) you want to copy it to.

3 Press `Tab` until you highlight the **File** area.

4 Press `↓` or `↑` until you highlight the file you want to copy (example: **TRAINING.LET**).

Note: To copy more than one file, select them in step 4. To select multiple files, refer to page 74.

5 Press `Alt`, `F`, `C` to select the **Copy** command.

◆ The **Copy File** dialog box appears.

6 Type the drive name, then type the path to the directory you want to copy the file to (example: **A:**).

Note: The \ stands for the root directory of the drive.

7 Press `Enter` to copy the file.

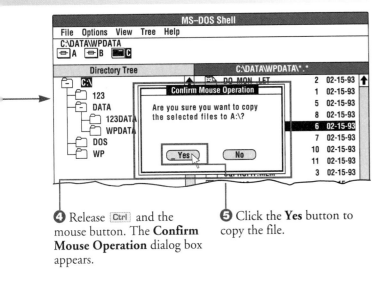

4 Release `Ctrl` and the mouse button. The **Confirm Mouse Operation** dialog box appears.

5 Click the **Yes** button to copy the file.

Rename a File

1 Press `Tab` until you highlight the **Directory Tree** area.

2 Press `↓` or `↑` until you highlight the directory that contains the file you want to rename (example: **123DATA**).

◆ The files in the highlighted directory appear.

3 Press `Tab` until you highlight the **File** area.

4 Press `↓` or `↑` until you highlight the file you want to rename (example: **INCOME3Q.WK1**).

5 Press `Alt`, `F`, `N` to select the **Rename** command.

Using the Mouse

1 Click the directory that contains the file you want to rename (example: **123DATA**).

2 Click the file you want to rename (example: **INCOME3Q.WK1**).

3 Click **File** to open its menu.

4 Click **Rename** and the **Rename File** dialog box appears.

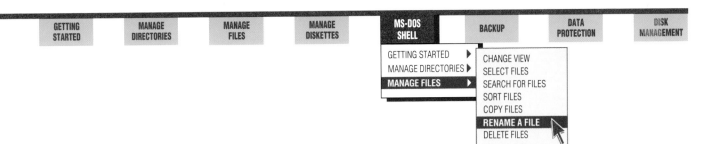

GETTING STARTED ▶
MANAGE DIRECTORIES ▶
MANAGE FILES ▶

CHANGE VIEW
SELECT FILES
SEARCH FOR FILES
SORT FILES
COPY FILES
RENAME A FILE
DELETE FILES

◆ The **Rename File** dialog box appears.

6 Type a new name for the file (example: **BUDGET3Q.WK1**) and then press **Enter**.

◆ The file is renamed.

5 Type a new name for the file (example: **BUDGET3Q.WK1**).

6 Click the **OK** button.

In this example, the INCOME3Q.WK1 file was renamed BUDGET3Q.WK1.

DELETE FILES

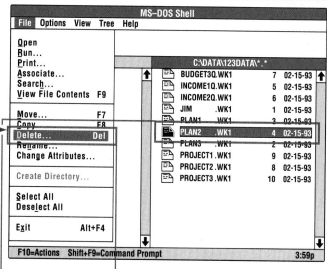

1 Press **Tab** until you highlight the **Directory Tree** area.

2 Press ↓ or ↑ until you highlight the directory that contains the file you want to delete (example: **123DATA**).

◆ The files in the highlighted directory appear.

3 Press **Tab** until you highlight the **File** area.

4 Press ↓ or ↑ until you highlight the file you want to delete (example: **PLAN2.WK1**).

*Note: To delete more than one file, select them in step **4**. To select multiple files, refer to page 74.*

5 Press **Alt**, **F**, **D** to select the **Delete** command.

Using the Mouse

❶ Click the directory that contains the file you want to delete (example: **123DATA**).

❷ Click the file you want to delete (example: **PLAN2.WK1**).

*Note: To delete more than one file, select them in step **❷**. To select multiple files, refer to page 74.*

❸ Click **File** to open its menu.

❹ Click **Delete** and the **Delete File Confirmation** dialog box appears.

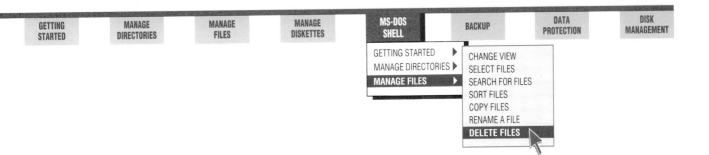

| GETTING STARTED | MANAGE DIRECTORIES | MANAGE FILES | MANAGE DISKETTES | MS-DOS SHELL | BACKUP | DATA PROTECTION | DISK MANAGEMENT |

GETTING STARTED ▶
MANAGE DIRECTORIES ▶
MANAGE FILES ▶

CHANGE VIEW
SELECT FILES
SEARCH FOR FILES
SORT FILES
COPY FILES
RENAME A FILE
DELETE FILES

◆ The **Delete File Confirmation** dialog box appears.

6 Press **Enter** to delete the file.

◆ The file is deleted.

5 Click the **Yes** button to delete the file.

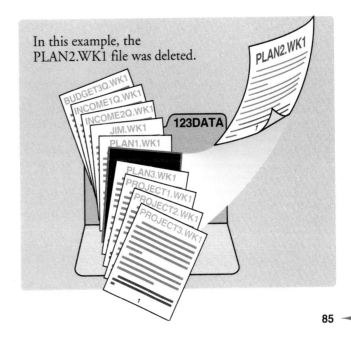

In this example, the PLAN2.WK1 file was deleted.

INTRODUCTION

PROTECT DATA

You can use Microsoft Backup to copy your files onto diskettes or other media. This way, you can replace lost data if your hard drive fails or you accidentally erase important files.

FREE UP HARD DISK SPACE

You can use Microsoft Backup to copy old or less-used files onto diskettes or other media. You can then remove these files from your hard drive to free disk space.

TRANSFER FILES TO ANOTHER COMPUTER

You can use Microsoft Backup to move your files to another computer.

Backup Media

Most of your program and data files are stored on your hard drive. You can use Microsoft Backup to copy these files to the following media:

DISKETTES

Diskettes are ideal for small backups (files totaling less than 20 megabytes).

NETWORK DRIVES

Network drives offer a secure environment for your backups. Ask your Network Administrator how to back up your files on a network.

OTHER MEDIA

Optical drives, removable hard disk cartridges and Bernoulli drives are practical for large backups (files totaling 20 megabytes or more).

Backup Schedule

Back up your work frequently. Ask yourself, "How much work can I afford to lose?" If it is only a day's worth, then make daily backups.

If your files do not often change during the week, back up weekly.

OCTOBER

Sun	Mon	Tues	Wed	Thurs	Fri	Sat
	1 •	2	3 •	4	5	6 •
7 •	8	9	10 •	11	12 •	13
14	15	16 •	17	18 •	19 •	20
21	22	23 •	24	25 •	26	27
28	29 •	30	31 •			

• *Back up on these days*

◆ Minimize your chances of losing important data by making at least two sets of backups.

Keep one set near your computer and the other set "off-site" in a safety-deposit box or in another building.

◆ Make a backup schedule and stick to it! Hard drive disasters always seem to happen right after you miss a scheduled backup.

INTRODUCTION
BACKUP SCHEDULE
START BACKUP
BACK UP YOUR FILES
RESTORE YOUR FILES

Start Microsoft Backup

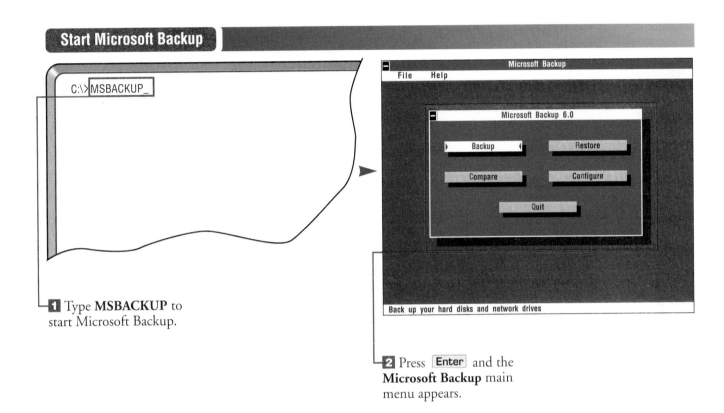

C:\>MSBACKUP_

1 Type **MSBACKUP** to start Microsoft Backup.

2 Press **Enter** and the **Microsoft Backup** main menu appears.

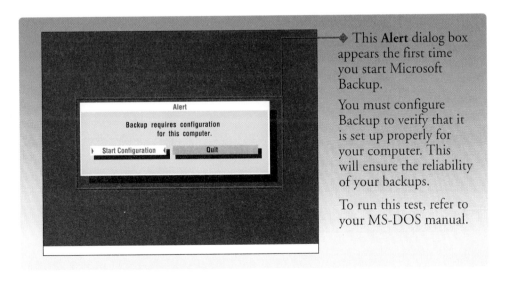

◆ This **Alert** dialog box appears the first time you start Microsoft Backup.

You must configure Backup to verify that it is set up properly for your computer. This will ensure the reliability of your backups.

To run this test, refer to your MS-DOS manual.

BACK UP YOUR FILES

1 Type **B** (for **B**ackup) and the **Backup** dialog box appears.

◆ The **Backup To:** box displays the size and type of diskette you will copy your files to.

*Note: To choose a different diskette, refer to **Change Backup Destination** below.*

2 Type **L** (for Select Files) and the **Select Backup Files** dialog box appears.

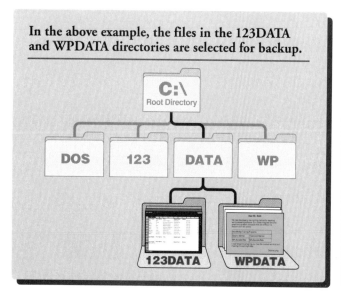

In the above example, the files in the 123DATA and WPDATA directories are selected for backup.

CHANGE BACKUP DESTINATION

1 Type **A** for (**B**ackup To:) and this dialog box appears.

2 Type the highlighted character corresponding to the diskette size and type you want to use.

3 Press **Enter**.

| GETTING STARTED | MANAGE DIRECTORIES | MANAGE FILES | MANAGE DISKETTES | MS-DOS SHELL | BACKUP | DATA PROTECTION | DISK MANAGEMENT |

INTRODUCTION
BACKUP SCHEDULE
START BACKUP
BACK UP YOUR FILES
RESTORE YOUR FILES

3 Press ⬇ until you highlight the directory containing the files you want to back up (example: **123DATA**).

◆ This area displays the files in the highlighted directory.

4 Press the **Spacebar** to select all the files in that directory. The files now display a check mark (✓) beside their names.

*Note: To deselect the files, press the **Spacebar** again.*

◆ To back up files in additional directories, repeat steps **3** and **4**.

◆ In this example, the files in the **WPDATA** directory are also selected for backup.

5 Press **Enter** to return to the **Backup** dialog box.

Microsoft Backup remembers the last files you backed up. The next time you want to back up the same data, you can eliminate steps **2** through **5**.

Step 2: Start the Backup

1 To start the Backup, type **S** (for **S**tart Backup).

◆ This indicates the number and type of diskettes needed.

◆ This indicates the number of files you selected for backup.

◆ This indicates the estimated backup time.

2 This **Alert** dialog box appears. Insert a diskette into the specified drive (example: **drive A**).

◆ The program displays the catalog for this backup.

3 Press **Enter** to begin the backup.

WHAT THE BACKUP CATALOG MEANS:

Each time you back up your files, the program creates a backup catalog. This catalog contains information about the files you are backing up. To restore files, you must know the backup catalog used.

◆ The drive backed up

◆ The backup date (month, day)

C C 3 02 18 A

◆ The last digit of the year

◆ Identifies multiple backups on the same day

◆ This **Alert** dialog box appears if you have inserted a diskette used for another backup.

4 To overwrite (replace) the files, type **O** (for **O**verwrite).

Note: To retain the files, use a new diskette.

5 If you require more than one diskette, follow the screen prompts for inserting them.

◆ The **Backup Complete** dialog box appears when the backup is complete.

◆ Check to ensure no files were skipped.

6 Press **Enter** to return to the **Microsoft Backup** main menu.

7 To return to the command prompt, type **Q** (for **Q**uit).

TIP

◆ Write the backup catalog on your diskette. If you use more than one diskette, number them sequentially.

RESTORE
YOUR FILES

You can restore lost data if your hard drive fails or you accidentally erase important information. The Restore feature copies the files from your backup diskettes to your hard drive.

Step 1: Select Catalog

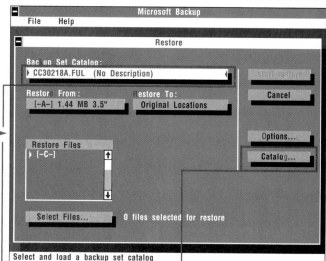

You must tell Microsoft Backup which catalog identifies the files you want to restore.

1 To start Microsoft Backup from the command prompt, type **MSBACKUP** and then press `Enter`.

2 Type `R` (for **R**estore) and the **Restore** dialog box appears.

◆ Microsoft Backup displays the catalog that identifies the files it will restore.

3 To restore a different catalog, type `G` (for Catalo**g**) and the **Select Catalog** dialog box appears.

INTRODUCTION
BACKUP SCHEDULE
START BACKUP
BACK UP YOUR FILES
RESTORE YOUR FILES

◆ The **Files** box displays the catalog names for all your backups. The catalog name identifying your last backup displays a check mark (✓) beside it.

4 Press ↓ or ↑ until you highlight the catalog that identifies the files you want to restore.

5 Press the **Spacebar** to select the catalog. A check mark (✓) appears beside it.

6 Press **Tab** twice to select **Load** and then press **Enter**.

◆ You are returned to the **Restore** dialog box.

◆ To restore your files, refer to the next page.

RESTORE YOUR FILES

1 Type **I** (for Restore Files) to select the **Restore Files** box.

2 Press the **Spacebar** to restore all files on the drive.

◆ Microsoft Backup indicates the number of files selected for restore.

Note: Backup created an extra file to store the catalog information.

◆ The **Restore From:** box displays the size and type of diskette you will restore your files from.

*Note: To choose a different diskette, refer to **Change Restore Source** below.*

3 Press **Tab** until you select **Start Restore** and then press **Enter**.

Before restoring your files, make sure you are ready to insert the diskettes. Check to ensure the diskettes contain the files you want to restore.

CHANGE RESTORE SOURCE

1 Press **Tab** until you select **Restore From:** and then press **Enter**. This dialog box appears.

2 Type the highlighted character corresponding to the diskette size and type you want to use.

3 Press **Enter**.

| GETTING STARTED | MANAGE DIRECTORIES | MANAGE FILES | MANAGE DISKETTES | MS-DOS SHELL | BACKUP | DATA PROTECTION | DISK MANAGEMENT |

INTRODUCTION
BACKUP SCHEDULE
START BACKUP
BACK UP YOUR FILES
RESTORE YOUR FILES

4 This **Alert** dialog box appears. Insert diskette #1 of the catalog you want to restore.

5 Press Enter to continue.

Note: If more than one diskette is required, follow the screen prompts for inserting them.

◆ The files are restored to your hard drive.

◆ Check to ensure no files were skipped.

6 Press Enter to return to the **Microsoft Backup** main menu.

7 To quit Microsoft Backup, type Q (for **Quit**).

DELETE OLD CATALOGS

Over time, you will accumulate a lot of catalog files. You can delete any catalog file you no longer require.

1 In the **Restore** dialog box, press Tab until you select **Catalog** and then press Enter.

2 Press ↑ or ↓ until you highlight the catalog you want to delete. Press the **Spacebar** to select it.

3 Press Tab until you select **Delete** and then press Enter.

4 This **Alert** dialog box appears. Press Enter to delete the catalog file.

DELETE SENTRY

Delete Sentry protects your data from permanent loss. Use it to restore files you have accidentally deleted.

Here's how it works...

◆ Delete Sentry is a small program you load into your computer's electronic memory. It watches for files being deleted.

SHOULD I USE DELETE SENTRY?

The advantage outweighs the disadvantages.

Advantage

◆ Delete Sentry can fully recover deleted files.

Disadvantages

◆ Delete Sentry requires 13.5K of memory.

◆ Delete Sentry can use up to 7% of your hard drive space.

◆ Delete Sentry only keeps deleted files for seven days.

| GETTING STARTED | MANAGE DIRECTORIES | MANAGE FILES | MANAGE DISKETTES | MS-DOS SHELL | BACKUP | DATA PROTECTION | DISK MANAGEMENT |

DELETE SENTRY
ANTI-VIRUS

◆ When you delete a file, Delete Sentry moves it to a special hidden directory called SENTRY.

◆ If you want to recover this file, Delete Sentry moves it back to its original location.

99

DELETE SENTRY

```
C:\>UNDELETE /SC/SA/SB_
```

```
C:\>UNDELETE /SC/SA/SB

UNDELETE - A delete protection facility
Copyright (C) 1987-1993 Central Point Software, Inc.
All rights reserved.

UNDELETE loaded.

Delete Protection Method is Delete Sentry.
Enabled for drives : A B C
```

You must install Delete Sentry on each drive you want to protect.

1 Type **UNDELETE** and then press the **Spacebar**.

2 Type **/S** (for **S**entry) followed by the letter of the drive you want to protect (example: drive **C**).

3 Repeat step **2** for each drive you want to protect (example: drives **A** and **B**).

4 Press **Enter** to install Delete Sentry on the drives you specified.

◆ When you install Delete Sentry, it automatically loads into electronic memory.

IMPORTANT!

You only need to **install** Delete Sentry once. However, you must **load** Delete Sentry each time you turn on your computer.

DELETE SENTRY
ANTI-VIRUS

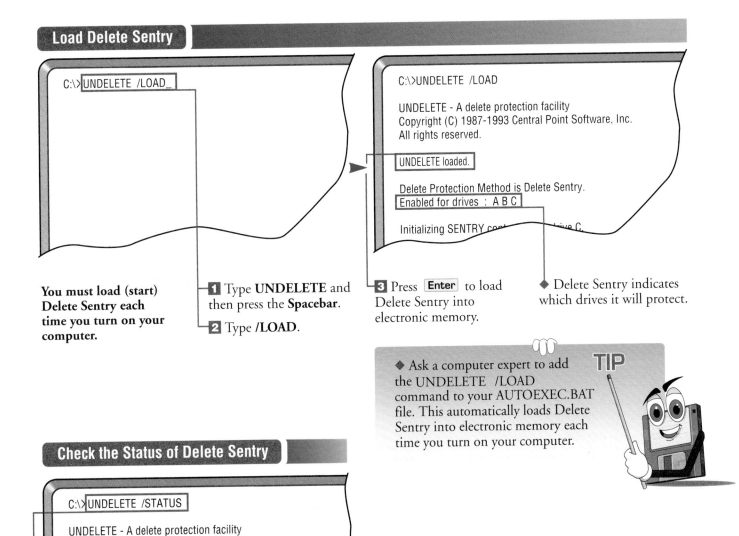

Load Delete Sentry

```
C:\>UNDELETE /LOAD_
```

```
C:\>UNDELETE /LOAD

UNDELETE - A delete protection facility
Copyright (C) 1987-1993 Central Point Software, Inc.
All rights reserved.

UNDELETE loaded.

Delete Protection Method is Delete Sentry.
Enabled for drives : A B C

Initializing SENTRY cont... ...rive C.
```

You must load (start) Delete Sentry each time you turn on your computer.

1 Type **UNDELETE** and then press the **Spacebar**.

2 Type **/LOAD**.

3 Press **Enter** to load Delete Sentry into electronic memory.

◆ Delete Sentry indicates which drives it will protect.

> **TIP**
>
> ◆ Ask a computer expert to add the UNDELETE /LOAD command to your AUTOEXEC.BAT file. This automatically loads Delete Sentry into electronic memory each time you turn on your computer.

Check the Status of Delete Sentry

```
C:\>UNDELETE /STATUS

UNDELETE - A delete protection facility
Copyright (C) 1987-1993 Central Point Software, Inc.
All rights reserved.

Delete Protection Method is Delete Sentry.
Enabled for drives : A B C

C:\>_
```

1 Type **UNDELETE** and then press the **Spacebar**.

2 Type **/STATUS**.

3 Press **Enter** and the current status of Delete Sentry appears.

DELETE SENTRY

Delete a File

```
C:\DATA\123DATA>DEL PLAN2.WK1

C:\DATA\123DATA>_
```

Before using the Delete command, make sure you load the Delete Sentry program.

1 Change to the directory that contains the file you want to delete.

Note: For example, to change to the \DATA\123DATA directory, type CD \DATA\123DATA and then press **Enter** *.*

2 Type **DEL** and then press the **Spacebar**.

3 Type the name of the file you want to delete (example: **PLAN2.WK1**) and then press **Enter** .

◆ Delete Sentry moves the file to a special hidden directory.

Recover Deleted Files

```
C:\DATA\123DATA>UNDELETE_
```

1 Change to the directory that originally contained the deleted files.

2 Type **UNDELETE** and then press **Enter** .

RECOVER ONE FILE

Use this method if you know the name of the file you want to recover.

1 Type **UNDELETE** and then press the **Spacebar**.

2 Type the name of the file you want to recover (example: **PLAN2.WK1**) and then press **Enter** .

3 Type **Y** (for **Y**es) to recover the file.

RECOVER ALL FILES AT THE SAME TIME

1 Type **UNDELETE** and then press the **Spacebar**.

2 Type **/ALL** and then press **Enter** .

GETTING STARTED	MANAGE DIRECTORIES	MANAGE FILES	MANAGE DISKETTES	MS-DOS SHELL	BACKUP	DATA PROTECTION	DISK MANAGEMENT

DELETE SENTRY
ANTI-VIRUS

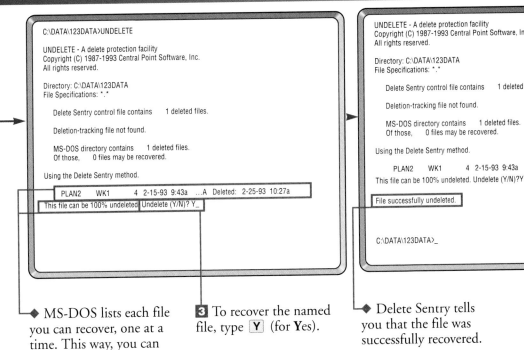

```
C:\DATA\123DATA>UNDELETE

UNDELETE - A delete protection facility
Copyright (C) 1987-1993 Central Point Software, Inc.
All rights reserved.

Directory: C:\DATA\123DATA
File Specifications: *.*

    Delete Sentry control file contains      1 deleted files.

    Deletion-tracking file not found.

    MS-DOS directory contains      1 deleted files.
    Of those,      0 files may be recovered.

Using the Delete Sentry method.

    PLAN2      WK1      4  2-15-93  9:43a  ...A  Deleted:  2-25-93  10:27a
This file can be 100% undeleted  Undelete (Y/N)? Y_
```

```
UNDELETE - A delete protection facility
Copyright (C) 1987-1993 Central Point Software, Inc.
All rights reserved.

Directory: C:\DATA\123DATA
File Specifications: *.*

    Delete Sentry control file contains      1 deleted files.

    Deletion-tracking file not found.

    MS-DOS directory contains      1 deleted files.
    Of those,      0 files may be recovered.

Using the Delete Sentry method.

    PLAN2      WK1      4  2-15-93  9:43a  ...A  Deleted:  2-25-93  10:27a
This file can be 100% undeleted. Undelete (Y/N)?Y

    File successfully undeleted.


C:\DATA\123DATA>_
```

◆ MS-DOS lists each file you can recover, one at a time. This way, you can decide which files you want to recover.

Note: Delete Sentry only keeps your deleted files for seven days. To lengthen or shorten this time period, ask a computer expert.

3 To recover the named file, type **Y** (for **Y**es).

◆ Delete Sentry tells you that the file was successfully recovered.

TIP

To free disk space, you can purge (permanently erase) all the files stored in Delete Sentry's hidden directory. Do this only after recovering all the files you need.

1 Type **UNDELETE** and then press the **Spacebar**.

2 Type **/PURGE** and then press **Enter**.

Note: This purges the files on the current drive.

103

ANTI-VIRUS

What are Computer Viruses?

Computer viruses are programs that multiply and spread to many computers without being detected.

Eventually, most viruses reveal their presence by displaying messages on the screen or by damaging files or entire hard drives.

MS-DOS includes two programs to protect your computer from viruses. They are: **MSAV** (Microsoft Anti-Virus) and **VSafe** (Virus Safe).

The VSafe and MSAV Partnership

Use both VSafe and MSAV for maximum protection against viruses.

◆ VSafe *continuously* checks for viruses and alerts you if it detects one. VSafe cannot destroy a virus. To remove a virus from your computer, use MSAV.

◆ MSAV detects and destroys viruses, but only when you instruct it to do so.

Note: New viruses are created every day. To protect your computer, periodically update your VSafe and MSAV programs. Consult your MS-DOS manual for more details.

VSafe   MSAV   VIRUS

| GETTING STARTED | MANAGE DIRECTORIES | MANAGE FILES | MANAGE DISKETTES | MS-DOS SHELL | BACKUP | DATA PROTECTION | DISK MANAGEMENT |

DELETE SENTRY
ANTI-VIRUS

How Viruses Infect Your Computer

DISKETTES

Viruses can hide inside programs stored on diskettes. They can also exist on diskettes that do not contain files. Four of the five most common viruses in the United States are spread by starting a computer with an infected diskette in a floppy drive.

MODEMS

Modems allow computers to transfer information over telephone lines. Viruses can attach themselves to the data being transferred and infect your computer. BBS's (Bulletin Board Systems) are particularly vulnerable.

NETWORKS

Networks link computers together to share data and programs. Viruses can quickly spread through a network. To protect your computer, ask your network administrator for virus protection information.

105

ANTI-VIRUS

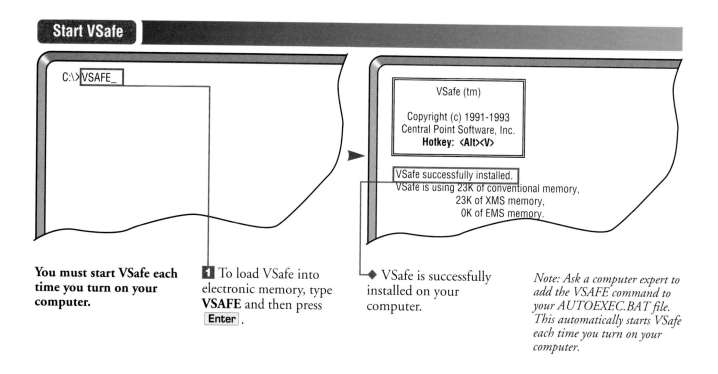

```
C:\>VSAFE_
```

```
         VSafe (tm)

     Copyright (c) 1991-1993
     Central Point Software, Inc.
       Hotkey:  <Alt><V>
```

VSafe successfully installed.
VSafe is using 23K of conventional memory,
23K of XMS memory,
0K of EMS memory.

You must start VSafe each time you turn on your computer.

1 To load VSafe into electronic memory, type **VSAFE** and then press `Enter`.

◆ VSafe is successfully installed on your computer.

Note: Ask a computer expert to add the VSAFE command to your AUTOEXEC.BAT file. This automatically starts VSafe each time you turn on your computer.

Virus Protection Plan

◆ Start VSafe immediately after turning on your computer.

◆ Use MSAV to check all new diskettes.

◆ Never start your computer with a diskette in a drive. If you accidentally do so, immediately use MSAV to check your computer.

◆ Use MSAV to check your hard drive at least once a month.

◆ If someone else uses your computer, use MSAV to check for viruses. This includes repair shops, friends and co-workers.

◆ Use MSAV to check your hard drive after receiving files through a modem.

| GETTING STARTED | MANAGE DIRECTORIES | MANAGE FILES | MANAGE DISKETTES | MS-DOS SHELL | BACKUP | DATA PROTECTION | DISK MANAGEMENT |

DELETE SENTRY
ANTI-VIRUS

Start MSAV

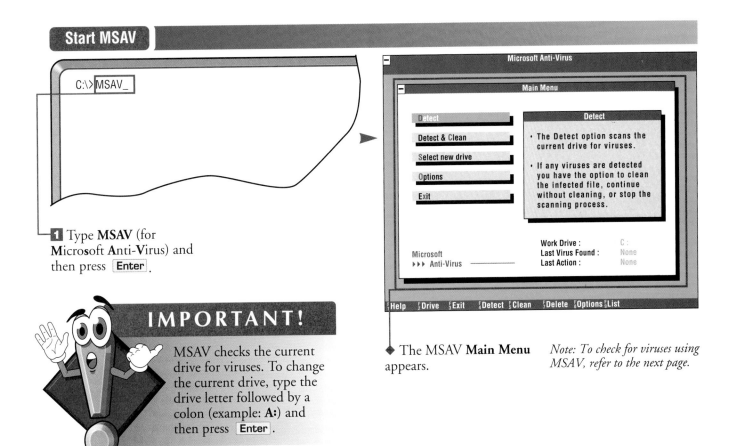

C:\> MSAV_

1 Type **MSAV** (for **M**icrosoft **A**nti-**V**irus) and then press **Enter**.

IMPORTANT!

MSAV checks the current drive for viruses. To change the current drive, type the drive letter followed by a colon (example: **A:**) and then press **Enter**.

◆ The MSAV **Main Menu** appears.

Note: To check for viruses using MSAV, refer to the next page.

ANTI-VIRUS

Check the Current Drive for Viruses

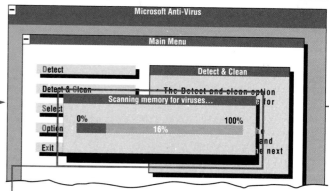

1 To check the current drive for viruses, type **C** (for Detect & **C**lean).

◆ The program checks your computer's electronic memory for viruses.

◆ If the program detects a virus, it automatically removes it.

Note: You can press **Esc** *to stop the program at any time.*

TIP ◆ You may never encounter a computer virus. In the odd chance you do, you now know how to detect and destroy it.

Exit MSAV

1 Type **X** (for E**x**it).

GETTING STARTED	MANAGE DIRECTORIES	MANAGE FILES	MANAGE DISKETTES	MS-DOS SHELL	BACKUP	DATA PROTECTION	DISK MANAGEMENT

DELETE SENTRY
ANTI-VIRUS

◆ The program then checks all your directories and files for viruses.

◆ If the program detects a virus, it automatically removes it.

◆ When the check is complete, the results appear.

◆ This column displays the number of disks and files checked.

◆ This column displays the number of disks and files cleaned.

◆ This column displays the number of disks and files infected by viruses.

Note: The number of infected disks and files should equal the number of cleaned disks and files. This tells you that your drive is virus free.

2 Press **Enter** to return to the **Main Menu**.

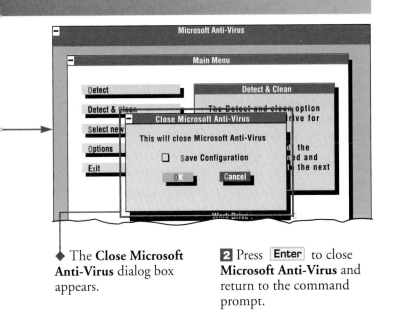

◆ The **Close Microsoft Anti-Virus** dialog box appears.

2 Press **Enter** to close **Microsoft Anti-Virus** and return to the command prompt.

SCANDISK

MS-DOS 6.2 includes ScanDisk, a new command that finds and repairs disk problems.

Start ScanDisk

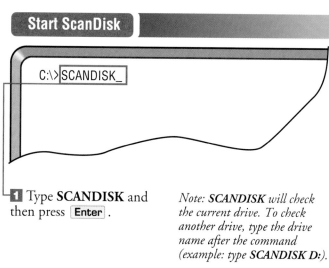

C:\> SCANDISK_

1 Type **SCANDISK** and then press **Enter**.

*Note: SCANDISK will check the current drive. To check another drive, type the drive name after the command (example: type **SCANDISK D:**).*

Using ScanDisk

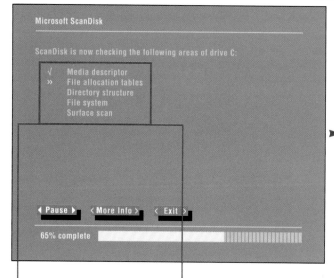

Microsoft ScanDisk

ScanDisk is now checking the following areas of drive C:

√ Media descriptor
» File allocation tables
  Directory structure
  File system
  Surface scan

◄ Pause ►   ‹ More Info ›   ‹ Exit ›

65% complete

Microsoft ScanDisk

ScanDisk has finished testing the file structure of drive C.

If you want, ScanDisk can also perform a surface scan on this drive. During a surface scan, ScanDisk checks the physical surface of the disk and identifies any areas that may be failing. In most cases, ScanDisk can recover the data from such areas.

A surface scan on drive C will take about 5 minutes. You can stop the scan at any time by choosing Exit.

Do you want to perform a surface scan now?

◄ Yes ►   ‹ No ›

◆ ScanDisk checks these areas of the drive.

◆ A check mark (✓) appears beside the area(s) that ScanDisk has checked.

◆ This message appears when ScanDisk has finished checking the file structure of the drive.

1 To perform a surface scan on the drive, type **Y** (for **Y**es).

*Note: If you do not want to perform a surface scan, type **N** (for **N**o).*

GETTING STARTED	MANAGE DIRECTORIES	MANAGE FILES	MANAGE DISKETTES	MS-DOS SHELL	BACKUP	DATA PROTECTION	DISK MANAGEMENT

SCANDISK
DOUBLESPACE
DEFRAGMENTER

SCANDISK versus CHECKDISK

ScanDisk can find and repair a much wider range of disk problems than CheckDisk (CHKDSK).

MS-DOS 6.0 Users

MS-DOS 6.0 does not provide the SCANDISK command. Use the CHKDSK /F command to find and correct disk problems.

MS-DOS 6.2 Users

Use the SCANDISK command instead of CHKDSK to find and correct disk problems.

TIP

◆ If ScanDisk finds a problem with the drive, a **Problem Found** dialog box will appear. To correct the problem, select the **Fix It** button.

◆ ScanDisk performs a surface scan on the drive.

◆ This message indicates the percentage of the drive that ScanDisk has checked.

◆ This message appears when the check is complete.

2 To return to the MS-DOS command prompt, type **X** (for Exit).

111

DOUBLESPACE

You can use DoubleSpace to compress the data stored on your hard drive. Your compressed drive will have 50 to 100 percent more free space.

Compression works by replacing long strings of characters with shorter strings.

For example, if "#" = "THE":

THEre THEy went to THE
(not compressed = 22 characters)

#re #y went to #
(compressed = 16 characters)

The compressed string of characters is almost 30% shorter.

| GETTING STARTED | MANAGE DIRECTORIES | MANAGE FILES | MANAGE DISKETTES | MS-DOS SHELL | BACKUP | DATA PROTECTION | DISK MANAGEMENT |

SCANDISK
DOUBLESPACE
DEFRAGMENTER

You only need to install DoubleSpace once. The program then works invisibly, compressing and decompressing your data.

◆ When you store new data on your hard drive, DoubleSpace automatically compresses it to reduce the amount of disk space required.

◆ When you use data stored on your hard drive, DoubleSpace automatically decompresses it.

TIP ◆ Everyone should use DoubleSpace to increase their hard drive capacity, especially those who have computers with limited disk space (example: portable computers).

Before Using DoubleSpace...

- ◆ Remove all floppy disks from your computer.
- ◆ Exit all programs.
- ◆ Back up your files. See pages 86-93 for more information.

DOUBLESPACE

`C:\> DBLSPACE_`

```
Microsoft DoubleSpace Setup

    Welcome to DoubleSpace Setup.

    The Setup program for DoubleSpace frees space on your hard
    disk by compressing the existing files on the disk. Setup
    also loads DBLSPACE.BIN, the portion of MS-DOS that provides
    access to DoubleSpace compressed drives. DBLSPACE.BIN
    requires about 40K of memory.

    If you use a network, then before installing DoubleSpace,
    start the network and connect to any drives you normally use.

      o To set up DoubleSpace now, press ENTER.

      o To learn more about DoubleSpace Setup, press F1.

      o To quit Setup without installing DoubleSpace, press F3.


ENTER=Continue   F1=Help   F3=Exit
```

1 Type **DBLSPACE**
(for **DoubleSpace**) and
then press `Enter`.

◆ The **Microsoft
DoubleSpace Setup**
screen appears.

2 Press `Enter` to set
up DoubleSpace.

*Note: To exit DoubleSpace,
press* `F3` *twice.*

◆ This screen appears
if you have already
installed DoubleSpace.

You only need to
install DoubleSpace
once. To return to the
MS-DOS prompt,
press `Alt`, `D`, `X`.

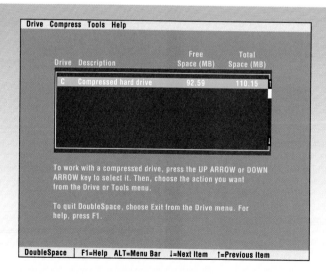

```
Drive  Compress  Tools  Help

                                           Free           Total
      Drive  Description                 Space (MB)     Space (MB)

        C    Compressed hard drive         92.59          110.15




To work with a compressed drive, press the UP ARROW or DOWN
ARROW key to select it. Then, choose the action you want
from the Drive or Tools menu.

To quit DoubleSpace, choose Exit from the Drive menu. For
help, press F1.

DoubleSpace   F1=Help  ALT=Menu Bar  ↓=Next Item  ↑=Previous Item
```

UNCOMPRESS A DRIVE

1 Before uncompressing a
drive, make sure you back
up the files on the drive.
To use Microsoft Backup,
refer to page 86.

*Note: If you are using MS-
DOS version 6.0, you cannot
uncompress a drive.*

2 Press `Alt`, `T`, `U` to
select the **Uncompress**
command.

3 To uncompress the
drive, press `Y` (for **Yes**).

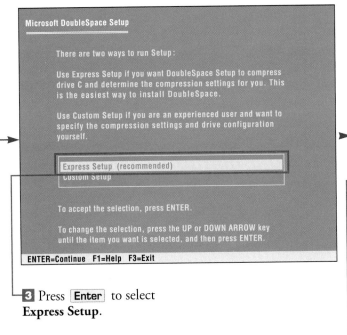

Microsoft DoubleSpace Setup

There are two ways to run Setup:

Use Express Setup if you want DoubleSpace Setup to compress drive C and determine the compression settings for you. This is the easiest way to install DoubleSpace.

Use Custom Setup if you are an experienced user and want to specify the compression settings and drive configuration yourself.

Express Setup (recommended)
Custom Setup

To accept the selection, press ENTER.

To change the selection, press the UP or DOWN ARROW key until the item you want is selected, and then press ENTER.

ENTER=Continue F1=Help F3=Exit

Microsoft DoubleSpace Setup

DoubleSpace is ready to compress drive C. This will take

┌─ Important ─┐

Before compressing this drive, you should back up the files it contains.

o To back up your files, choose Exit, and then run Microsoft Backup. For more informatino, press F1.

o To compress this drive now, choose Continue.

< Exit > <Continue> < Help >

C=Continue F1=Help F3=Exit ESC=Previous screen

3 Press **Enter** to select **Express Setup**.

◆ DoubleSpace indicates you should back up the files on the drive before compressing the drive.

◆ If you have not backed up your files, press **E** (for **E**xit) to return to the command prompt. Then use Microsoft Backup to back up your files. Refer to page 86 for more information.

4 To compress the drive now, press **C** (for **C**ontinue).

Note: Refer to the next page to continue the DoubleSpace Setup process.

F1 Press **F1** to receive help on DoubleSpace.

F3 Press **F3** twice to exit DoubleSpace.

DOUBLESPACE

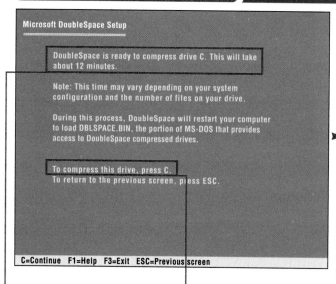

Microsoft DoubleSpace Setup

DoubleSpace is ready to compress drive C. This will take about 12 minutes.

Note: This time may vary depending on your system configuration and the number of files on your drive.

During this process, DoubleSpace will restart your computer to load DBLSPACE.BIN, the portion of MS-DOS that provides access to DoubleSpace compressed drives.

To compress this drive, press C.
To return to the previous screen, press ESC.

C=Continue F1=Help F3=Exit ESC=Previous screen

Microsoft DoubleSpace Setup

DoubleSpace is now compressing drive C.

Start time: 1:42:45pm
Current time: 1:45:15pm
Estimated finish time: 1:56pm

Time left: About 11 minutes.

Currently Compressing: C:\DOS\LABEL.EXE

20% complete

Compressing files...

◆ DoubleSpace is ready to compress drive C. It displays the estimated time required to compress the drive (example: 12 minutes).

Note: To exit DoubleSpace, press **F3** *twice.*

5 Press **C** to compress the drive.

◆ DoubleSpace will run ScanDisk to check for problems on your drive.

◆ When ScanDisk finishes checking your drive, DoubleSpace starts compressing the data.

◆ This indicates the percentage of data on your hard drive compressed by DoubleSpace.

◆ This indicates the estimated time left.

DoubleSpace compresses the data on your hard drive to increase its storage capacity.

GETTING STARTED	MANAGE DIRECTORIES	MANAGE FILES	MANAGE DISKETTES	MS-DOS SHELL	BACKUP	DATA PROTECTION	DISK MANAGEMENT

SCANDISK
DOUBLESPACE
DEFRAGMENTER

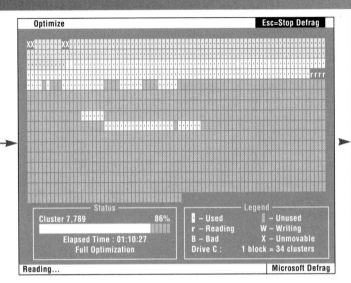

```
Optimize                                    Esc=Stop Defrag

XXX          XXX



                                                      rrrr



┌──────── Status ────────┐  ┌──────── Legend ────────┐
│ Cluster 7,789      86% │  │ ▓ – Used    ░ – Unused │
│                        │  │ r – Reading  W – Writing│
│ Elapsed Time : 01:10:27│  │ B – Bad      X – Unmovable│
│    Full Optimization   │  │ Drive C :  1 block = 34 clusters│
└────────────────────────┘  └────────────────────────┘
Reading...                                 Microsoft Defrag
```

```
Microsoft DoubleSpace Setup
────────────────────────────

DoubleSpace has finished compressing drive C.

┌────────────────────────────────────────────────┐
│ Free space before compression :   42.4 MB       │
│ Free space after compression :    89.0 MB       │
│ Compression ratio :               1.5 to 1      │
│ Total time to compress :          12 minutes.   │
│                                                  │
│ DoubleSpace has created a new drive H that contains 2.0 MB │
│ of uncompressed space. This space has been set aside for  │
│ files that must remain uncompressed.             │
└────────────────────────────────────────────────┘

┌────────────────────────────────────────────────┐
│ To exit from DoubleSpace and restart your computer, press │
│ ENTER.                                           │
└────────────────────────────────────────────────┘



ENTER=Continue
```

◆ When DoubleSpace finishes compressing your hard drive, it defragments your files.

◆ The defragmenting process reorganizes the files stored on your hard drive to optimize disk performance.

◆ Once DoubleSpace completes the defragmenting process, it displays information about your compressed drive.

6 Press **Enter** to exit DoubleSpace and restart your computer.

◆ You may now use your hard drive as usual.

DoubleSpace then defragments your hard drive to improve its efficiency.

Note: For more information on defragmenting your hard drive, refer to page 118.

◆ Your compressed drive will have 50 to 100 percent more free space.

DEFRAGMENTER

HOW MS-DOS STORES YOUR FILES

Inside the case of your hard drive is a stack of platters called disks. These disks magnetically store your data files.

When you save a file to your hard drive, MS-DOS stores it in one or more storage spaces called "clusters." MS-DOS tries to keep together all the clusters of a file by placing them in adjacent spaces. This way, your computer can retrieve a file quickly and efficiently.

◆ **cluster**

◆ **one file**

Eventually, you will delete files from your hard drive. This leaves empty spaces between the remaining files.

WHY DO FILES FRAGMENT?

Sometimes, MS-DOS cannot find enough adjacent empty spaces to store an entire file. It must then break the file apart and store the fragments in empty spaces all over the disk. This process is called disk fragmentation.

Note: Files may also fragment when you add additional information to them.

| GETTING STARTED | MANAGE DIRECTORIES | MANAGE FILES | MANAGE DISKETTES | MS-DOS SHELL | BACKUP | DATA PROTECTION | DISK MANAGEMENT |

SCANDISK
DOUBLESPACE
DEFRAGMENTER

Before and After Defragmenting

BEFORE DEFRAGMENTING

A fragmented disk contains files that are broken up and scattered around it. When MS-DOS wants to retrieve a file, it must search the entire disk to find all the fragments of that file.

Fragmentation does not alter the information stored on your hard drive, but it does reduce performance speed.

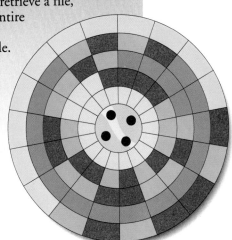

AFTER DEFRAGMENTING

Defragmenter places all the clusters of each file together. This reduces the time your hard drive requires to retrieve a file.

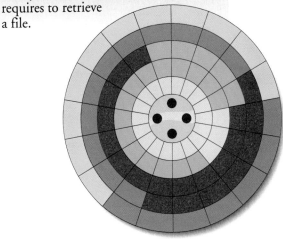

Sort Files During Defragmentation

When you defragment the files on your hard drive, you can also sort them by name, extension, date or size (in ascending or descending order). This can make it easier for you to find your data files.

Note: Any new files you add to the computer after using the Defragmenter will not appear "sorted."

Z_FILE.LET
TRAINING.LET
NOTE1Q.TXT
MERGE.LET
DO_MON.LET
AGENDA.TXT

WPDATA

◆ These files are sorted by name in ascending order.

DEFRAGMENTER

Defragment Files on Your Hard Drive (C:)

IMPORTANT!

◆ Use Defragmenter at least twice a month.

◆ Do not turn off or reset your computer while running Defragmenter.

◆ Before using Defragmenter:

▸ Exit all programs, including Windows.

▸ Run **SCANDISK** as described on page 110.

DEFRAGMENT WITHOUT SORTING FILES

```
C:\>DEFRAG C: /F_
```

1 Type **DEFRAG** and then press the **Spacebar**.

2 Type **C:** and then press the **Spacebar**.

3 Type **/F** (for **F**ragment) and then press Enter.

DEFRAGMENT AND SORT FILES BY NAME (A TO Z)

```
C:\>DEFRAG C: /F /SN_
```

1 Type **DEFRAG** and then press the **Spacebar**.

2 Type **C:** and then press the **Spacebar**.

3 Type **/F** (for **F**ragment) and then press the **Spacebar**.

4 Type **/SN** (for **S**ort by **N**ame) and then press Enter.

Defragment and sort files by name (Z to A)

Type **DEFRAG C: /F /SN–**

DEFRAGMENT AND SORT FILES BY EXTENSION (A TO Z)

```
C:\>DEFRAG C: /F /SE_
```

1 Type **DEFRAG** and then press the **Spacebar**.

2 Type **C:** and then press the **Spacebar**.

3 Type **/F** (for **F**ragment) and then press the **Spacebar**.

4 Type **/SE** (for **S**ort by **E**xtension) and then press Enter.

Defragment and sort files by extension (Z to A)

Type **DEFRAG C: /F /SE–**

GETTING STARTED	MANAGE DIRECTORIES	MANAGE FILES	MANAGE DISKETTES	MS-DOS SHELL	BACKUP	DATA PROTECTION	**DISK MANAGEMENT**

SCANDISK
DOUBLESPACE
DEFRAGMENTER

DEFRAGMENT AND SORT FILES BY DATE (EARLIEST FIRST)

C:\> DEFRAG C: /F /SD_

1 Type **DEFRAG** and then press the **Spacebar**.

2 Type **C:** and then press the **Spacebar**.

3 Type **/F** (for **F**ragment) and then press the **Spacebar**.

4 Type **/SD** (for **S**ort by **D**ate) and then press Enter .

Defragment and sort files by date (latest first)

Type **DEFRAG C: /F /SD–**

DEFRAGMENT AND SORT FILES BY SIZE (SMALLEST FIRST)

C:\> DEFRAG C: /F /SS_

1 Type **DEFRAG** and then press the **Spacebar**.

2 Type **C:** and then press the **Spacebar**.

3 Type **/F** (for **F**ragment) and then press the **Spacebar**.

4 Type **/SS** (for **S**ort by **S**ize) and then press Enter .

Defragment and sort files by size (largest first)

Type **DEFRAG C: /F /SS–**

Defragmenter reorganizes the files stored on your hard drive to optimize disk performance.

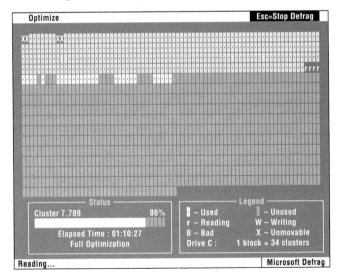

If you install DoubleSpace before running Defragmenter, this screen appears.

Please wait
Now starting the DoubleSpace program
to defragment your compressed drive
DoubleSpace is defragmenting drive C. To interrupt it,
DoubleSpace is remounting drive C.
DoubleSpace has finished defragmenting drive C.

C:\>_

INDEX